I Begin Again

I
Begin Again

By ALICE BRETZ

Whittlesey House
MCGRAW-HILL BOOK CO.
New York   *London*

PUBLISHED BY WHITTLESEY HOUSE

A division of the McGraw-Hill Book Company, Inc.

Printed in the United States of America by the Maple Press Co., York, Pa.

To

HAROLD CAILE

who understands what has
been lost, what gained

Acknowledgment

My thanks to the American Foundation for the
Blind for its unstinted help, and particularly
to Miss Enid Griffis for her editing of this book.

A. B.

Foreword

Some time ago three articles about Mrs. Bretz by Frederick Woltman appeared in the N. Y. World-Telegram. When the linotype operator had finished putting them in type, he turned to the man next to him and said, "This is the most interesting story I have ever set up."

It is highly probable that readers across the country will paraphrase the comment of the printer and say, "This is the most interesting story I have ever read."

It is not difficult to find the reason. Whether we are hard-boiled newspapermen, professional workers in varied fields, children at play, or old folk in the chimney corner, we all react alike to a story of courage. I have gone through this book many times, and find that the quality of courage shines implicit from every page. Side by side with that courage one encounters humor and gaiety. Somehow, all three combine to make me think of a verse by an Australian poet, A. L. Gordon:

> Life is mostly froth and bubble;
> Two things stand like stone:
> Kindness in another's trouble;
> Courage in your own.

It is hardly letting the cat out of the bag to say that the trouble which caused Alice Bretz to begin again was stone blindness which came to her suddenly in adult life. Revealing that fact does not reveal the story. In the following pages she herself has done that with a feeling for drama, a depth of emotion, and a narrative sweep that carries the reader with her along the whole gallant course.

When I read the book in manuscript, I suggested to Mrs. Bretz that she give it the title "Singing in the Dark," but she decided otherwise. With the writer's usual tenacity, I still prefer the title which I gave her. Whistling in the dark, as we all know, is an attempt to keep up one's spirits. Singing in the dark is only possible when one's spirit has soared above the shadows, overcome fear, and established a victorious serenity.

Probably Mrs. Bretz turned down the suggestion because she felt it had a Pollyanna ring to it.

Certainly she has little in common with that beguiling escapist. Pollyanna, if you remember, faced the world with a smile because she refused to face facts. Mrs. Bretz has faced facts, and still continues to smile. She has created for herself a successful working philosophy which radiates without the aid of synthetic sunshine.

Alice Bretz's story is a success story—the achievement of a self-contained, independent life against unusual odds. To John Milton's question, "Doth God demand day labor, light denied?" Mrs. Bretz has answered "Yes," and in so answering has lost neither her faith nor her fortitude. We are fortunate to have this record set down by her in this inspiring human document.

F. Fraser Bond.

I Begin Again

Chapter 1

The earliest guests to arrive were a brother and sister. The man knew our house, but it was his sister's first visit, and her greeting ended with an exclamation, "What a lovely room!" I smiled at our new guest as she sank into a wing chair beside the fireplace, and her gray chiffon dress billowed as would a puff of smoke. I watched her gaze travel, and, thus guided, my eyes saw the room anew.

An impact of color stirred me. It was like the opening chord of an overture. Then, the way different instruments would take their places, separate objects came into view.

The rose, violet, and gold of the various lampshades harmonized or accented the simple scheme of decoration. Light flooded the room, sparkled on polished wood. Brass andirons radiated a firelike brilliance from leaping flames. Other pieces of brass held dancing light beams on their surfaces. A Chinese rug with its scarlet and blue looked like a giant thirteenth century French missal lying open on the floor. The window draperies had been drawn, and the orange splashes in their design winked at me like twinkling stars in a midnight-blue sky.

Between the windows, the purple of asters in a vase was deepened in tone by the violet-shaded lamp standing near by. In the southeast corner of the room, a jar of orange and yellow zinnias held golden light. A scarlet cocktail cushion came into unexpected prominence, as though it were made of Chinese lacquer, and called a greeting to the rug. My glance was caught by gold letters written in light on the red, blue, and green bindings in the bookcase. Mirrors had become pictures of great beauty, multiplying vivid colors and spots of light.

My guest was right. The room was "lovely," and its cheer and color added to the happiness of our friends.

The last guest had gone, and I stood looking at the room, empty now, except for light and color. The soft rose-purple glow of a samovar caught my eyes. Everywhere there were touches of color—some rich and bright, some dull and subdued. I love color. It pulsates with life. The room was still alive.

I turned out the light. The room was dark. The color vanished. I stood there amid strange surroundings. I knew that I must go through the doorway on the opposite side of the room. Where was it? There was no opposite, in the dark. What would I stumble against on my way? Well, it was silly to stand there, feeling the uncanniness of darkness. All I had to do would be to switch on the light. Suppose . . . suppose there were no light!

* * * * *

It was a sunny morning, and I was returning from the woods on our farm, my arms filled with dogwood blossoms. The tree couldn't be seen from our house, for it grew hidden among tall hickory, black walnut, and beech trees. I had found it on an early walk over the farm, and every spring brought branches of white flowers to decorate the living room. The dogwood liked my admiration and gave generously of its treasures. The blossoms were unusually large that year, and their whiteness was dazzling when I carried them into the sunshine.

Beyond the wood, I looked at the shining bright greenness of May. The leaves of trees and plants mingled their differing greens in glamorous brilliance. I looked up. The sky was dotted with clouds, like spattered stiffly beaten egg whites. I paused at the edge of a wheat field. The vigorous stools were a healthy green and promised a rich harvest. On one corner of the field lay the shadow of a cloud. The cloud would slowly drift. The shadow would spread until it covered the whole field. Suppose . . .

Suppose a shadow covered the sun forever—darkness everywhere. I would stand there lost, unable even to see the dogwood blossoms close to my face.

* * * * *

The zenith of the sunny day was the farm. And the farm was the fulfillment of a dream.

My husband and I were city people, and, like others who live in walled streets, we longed for and talked of the country. At last we decided to buy a farm.

The choice of a location was the next step. I read books and magazines about country life. Since we were New Yorkers, our first thought was Connecticut. Views were lovely, stone walls romantic, but I assured the real estate man who was pointing out the beauty that views could not be farmed and that small fields bounded by stone were impractical for a tractor.

My husband had consented to the tractor idea when I said, "I know nothing about horses, and a hired man might not feed the animals properly, or something. And the poor creatures would suffer. But if a tractor were mistreated, only our bank account would be hurt." My husband knew all about horses, but his medical work occupied his time, and he planned to be at home only week ends.

A farm in Massachusetts attracted us. Fortunately, or unfortunately, I asked a neighbor about the growing season. She said, "Snow flies about the first of November. It piles high over the shutters of the lower windows. You can be pretty sure of spring in June." We didn't buy in Massachusetts because I wanted a long growing season. And in Virginia I was told that I couldn't actually work in the garden. Negroes did that. So we dropped Virginia from our list.

Our ignorance of farming was abysmal. Through train windows we had glimpsed men plowing. At other seasons we'd seen corn in shocks, covering a field with wigwams, and haystacks standing deserted. How such things were done we had no idea, and it seemed to me that before buying a farm, one of us should know something at least of the theory of farming. Since Dr. Bretz was too busy to study agriculture, I went to Columbia University. There I was taught many practical things, but one important item of information was not included in the curriculum. I learned it later. This essential bit of information is that a farmer thinks that a woman doesn't know anything, particularly a city woman who has learned out of books.

After a five-year hunt, we found the perfect place, in New Jersey. We moved in the last of June and started at once to get the place ready for the next spring.

I hired local carpenters to fix the house, and they promptly wrecked all the rooms. I told them what I wanted, but they didn't follow directions. I fired them and hired a gang from a distance. The new group included masons and plumbers. Dr. Bretz wanted a porch, and I wanted a bathroom. The porch proved to be cheaper. We have never owned an industry, but it seemed to me that our weekly pay roll was like that of a factory.

While workmen swarmed over the house, I examined the farm, foot by foot. There are a great many feet in 153 acres, and I was kept busy. Boundary fences would have to be mended and certain portions rebuilt. Steve Danbury, the local handyman, took care of this. When he put in the posts for a boundary fence and could find neither man nor boy to help string the barbed wire, I became his assistant. We carried the spool of wire on an iron rod between us. It was so heavy that, at first, I could walk only about eight steps. Danbury was smart, however, and we walked downhill. As the spool unrolled, I could walk a greater distance. The fronts of my legs, above the knees, were black and blue from pressing against the iron bar, but the fence was finished. A few weeks later, I showed my husband how to use a wire stretcher. He and I finished the fence around the apple orchard. We didn't use barbed wire, and perhaps our workmanship was not so good as Danbury's, but it looked all right.

The twenty-two-acre pasture had great patches of Canada thistles, and I had read somewhere that if thistles were cut down while in green bud, not only would those plants be destroyed but there would be no seeds. Whereupon I bought a sickle.

The proprietor of the hardware store asked me if I knew how to use it. On learning of my ignorance, he explained, "You must stand with your right leg forward and hold your left hand on your left knee to keep the hand from swinging out and being cut by the sweeping curve of the sickle." To illustrate, he showed me his own left hand, with the forefinger missing.

With these instructions and the example of the crippled hand in mind, I went to the pasture on a hot August afternoon and slew a lot of thistles.

In the midst of the carnage, I came near a flat rock where, surrounded by a lusty thistle phalanx standing guard, a shining black snake sunned himself. Snakes give me the shivers, which, even on a hot day, I am incapable of appreciating. At this moment it seemed time to go home. I stood frozen and looked at the ugly creature. If those thistles were allowed to go to seed, the rest of my work would be wasted. If a snake drove me out of the field, I would never go there again for fear of meeting him. But the black snake slithered off the rock at my approach, and the thistles fell under my sickle in record time.

The thistle-cutting and the fence-building stories spread through the neighborhood, and, while the farm women thought me odd, they became very friendly.

The farm wasn't all work. There was beauty, lavish beauty, in it and in its surroundings. Our circular view showed gently rolling hills and shallow, well-watered valleys. To the east there was a higher range of hills covered with cedar, and a long distance to the west was a similar range. These two ranges were called mountains. How high must a hill be before it's a mountain? I had seen moonlight on the Jungfrau many times—it was glorious. But there was a cozier thrill when a winter dawn turned the cedars on the east ridge into Spanish lace. Included in the view were many prosperous farms, with neatly painted white houses and red barns.

The seasons provided their own individual loveliness. The great expanse of winter sky was brilliant with stars, friendly and near. I saw my first sight of winter sky untouched by Edison, and I found its glory amazing. The moon, too, had plenty of space to sail in. We could watch the new moon for hours. The full moon spilled enchantment over the earth. Thunderstorms were fascinating. Clouds would gather at different points on the horizon, their rendezvous being a spot right over our heads. There they clashed and roared, and threw bright, slashing spears of lightning. There was the richness wrought by the seasons on fruit trees and gardens. And, occasionally, an extra thrill, as when the setting sun threw long streamers of light across a November flower bed, all brown and wet, touching a cock pheasant into flaming glory.

Light and color are the life of the world, and I was most conscious of this in the spring. On one sunny day in mid-April, everywhere I looked, the living beauty around me made my blood tingle in response to its stimulant. The plum trees were fat little white clouds tethered to sticks, the bank of daffodils yellower than the sun. Inside, the house was gay with fresh flowers.

The vegetable garden showed several rows of green which would grow in the warm sunshine. I looked at the iris bed, and pictured it blooming in the next few weeks. The plants would be healthier if I pulled out the grass that had crept in from the lawn. I love weeding, for the sight of an orderly garden is so satisfying. All my gardens were never weedless at the same time. The patch I weeded on Monday would have new weeds the following Monday. The earth was generous. The sun shone warmly on flowers and weeds alike.

I knelt to weed the iris bed. The sun was hot, the spring air full of the intangible fragrance of budding leaves. The earth was softly damp. The iris roots seemed grateful to be freed from creeping grass. Hours passed unnoticed.

My housekeeper, Mrs. Baldwin, came out bringing a package of cigarettes. "Isn't it time for you to stop for a smoke, Mrs. Bretz?" The suggestion was welcome and, as the grass was too damp for me to sit down, I tried to stand. To my amazement, and amusement, my knees refused their support. They lay on the ground, as flat as noodles on a plate. There was no pain, no tingling as though they had been asleep. Mrs.

Baldwin was not strong enough, nor tall enough, to be of any assistance. The predicament made me laugh. The porch was fifty feet away, and I crept to it across the grass, on hands and knees. I pulled myself up on the steps and let my legs dangle. The knees were still "noodle-ish." I lighted a cigarette, and by the time I had finished smoking it, my legs were behaving properly. At Mrs. Baldwin's suggestion, I walked into the living room and lay down on the couch.

That afternoon I told the little incident to a Flemington friend who had dropped in for tea. She advised a doctor, insisting my experience was very unusual and might indicate some serious condition, but I refused to be scared and said I would wait for several days until Dr. Bretz returned from Indianapolis. This friend was not satisfied, and telephoned my son. He promptly appeared with an excellent doctor, who thumped me all over and said, though I felt perfectly well, "It must be some kind of poison."

Later, this doctor and my husband had a consultation, and took blood tests. I went in to New York, and more doctors thumped and took more blood tests and said it was "a poison," but they didn't know what. Finally, Dr. Hyslop thumped, like the others, and said, "Thyroid."

I returned to the farm. Four months of rest and treatment followed before we came to New York to stay near doctors. There wasn't any goiter. There wasn't any pain, until the light began to hurt my eyes. I lost twenty pounds, and my heart jumped around. This doesn't sound like a professional diagnosis—it is only the way it seemed to me.

Another four months of treatment in the city, with the hospital as the last resort. It was Christmas time, and the word "resort" made me think of Atlantic City.

Chapter 2

Hospitals had never appeared attractive to me. Their stiff starchiness was as rigid and cold as steel. Their cold whiteness was reminiscent of a cemetery, where figures in hard glistening uniforms played Moving-day for Tombstones. I had never been a hospital patient, and my casual acquaintance with such institutions had consisted in visiting unfortunate friends. Yet when the occasion arose for me to go to one for a short stay, the fact had to be faced and my dislike pushed into the background.

An operation on a thyroid gland is quite commonplace and in my case would be simple, since there was no goiter. I went to the hospital prepared to stay ten days. . . . Four months later I recovered a lasting consciousness.

The serious turn to my illness surprised even the doctors, and its graver aspect was unexpected, although I was ignorant of this at the time. The doctors may have considered my ignorance a blessing and thought that there would be no necessity to enlighten me, for six times during the months of unconsciousness, interspersed with days of awareness, they said I was dying.

I was ignorant of these six episodes, and on a day after one of them, when I was conscious, a scene incomprehensible to me took place in my room. A young interne came in on his morning round. I wish that I could remember his name; he was a nice young doctor. I asked the nurse to give him a glass of port. He took the wine and said, "What is the toast, Mrs. Bretz?"

My reply should have been, "To my quick recovery," or some equally commonplace remark. Instead I whispered, "To the bankruptcy of the undertakers."

Silence followed, and the nice young doctor left the room without speaking. The nurse told me that his eyes had filled with tears and that he had put down the glass untasted. Later I learned that the preceding night he had watched me while they thought I was dying.

I had entered the hospital a day or two after Christmas, and it was well into April before my thoughts became consecutive. The knowledge that it was April came as a surprise—a pleasant one, for it meant spring.

I talked to the nurse about our farm, and in my enthusiasm the dark room and the bandage on my face were forgotten. "Dr. Bretz and I are keen about farming," I told her. "We left a man and wife on the place to take care of it while we are in town." Had they planted the early vegetables? I wondered—had the twenty acres of oats been put in, to be followed with a catch crop of buckwheat? I prattled on. There would be timothy to be cut in the summer. There would be no wheat this year because I had been too sick last fall to think about the wheat, timothy, clover mixture. Dr. Bretz didn't know anything about the running of the farm, although he always helped if there was anything being done on Friday afternoon or Saturday when he was home. We would have to buy wheat for the chickens—had the twelve hundred baby chicks been bought to replenish the stock—had the orchards been pruned and sprayed and the grape vines carefully tied?

I talked about my gardens—the thousand yellow daffodils on the small terrace sloping from the lawn to the drive must be in full bloom— there was a mat of wild blue violets beside the pasture gate—the fragrant white violets that nestled under the box hedge were probably through blooming. I described the flower bed that bordered the lawn, it was 150 feet long and almost filled with perennials, although there were spaces for annuals—there were purple asters with crimson stems and ostrich-plumed ones in lavender and white—there was a space, too, for the little yellow French marigolds and the gorgeously colored giant zinnias. I must get back to the garden because only I knew where the plants would come up—the blue anchusa, peonies, scarlet Oriental poppies, lupins, columbines, chrysanthemums, and a host of others, all of which I had planted and cared for.

The nurse and I heard Dr. Rogers in the hall, and she hurried away to meet him. My mind was full of happiness, the picture of the garden was so vivid with its gay colors that my fingers felt for the warm earth and touched a blanket. I must get well soon. I had had no experience with sickness but vaguely remembered that a patient had to walk around the room for several days before leaving a hospital—I would ask the doctor this very morning if I could get up—I might manage to be on the farm by the first of May—the apple trees would be in blossom, their rose-tipped white petals making the orchard another heavenly garden. My breath came in an ecstatic gasp remembering their beauty.

My heart was so full of joy that I had been unaware of the doctor's presence until he spoke.

"Nurse tells me that you are planning to go back to your farm. You can't. You're blind."

My first thought came in words. "Thank you, doctor. That must have been a difficult thing to say." The second thought followed quickly and I didn't speak. He had said that about *me*—my husband, my son—a blind wife and mother. It was incredible. This thing couldn't have happened to me.

I lay very still, no one spoke, perhaps the doctor and nurse had left me alone. There was something horrible in the room waiting to touch me if I moved, a fearful, slimy creature quite near my face. I didn't dare put up my hand. The hopeless struggle was like a nightmare—only this wasn't a dream, it was real. It would last for the rest of my life. A ghastly thing crouched on my bed—it would spring on me—I held myself tense and rigid, afraid that my very breathing might attract the attention of the Thing. Horror filled my mind—hours passed.

A clergyman came to the hospital to see me. I was too dazed to follow his quiet, gentle voice, or what he was saying. Then a sentence cut through to my consciousness: "My child, God has laid His cross upon you." The words were a blistering iron on my quivering nerves. I felt an

enormous cross laid on my back and shoulders;
its weight bore me to the ground; I lay with my
face in the dust—tired, oh, so tired, I could never
move again. It made no difference. I was crushed.
Then, slowly, dimly, at a great distance, I saw
the church I had attended as a child and where I
had been confirmed; I saw the choir boys coming
from the vestry room; I heard them singing
"Onward, Christian Soldiers." I couldn't distinguish the words except "With the Cross of
Jesus going on before." The cross going on before!
These boys and men were not carrying the cross
on their backs; their shoulders were not bowed
under its weight. Their heads were up, their
voices triumphant; they followed the cross singing. I saw the pale gold gleam of the cross held
high above their heads; the uplifted cross was
their leader. Something stirred within me. The
cross was a symbol of courage and not a heavy
burden; the words kept repeating themselves, "a
symbol of courage." My body lay flat on its back,
but I wasn't thinking of it, not even of my blind
eyes. I was praying, praying not in the beautiful
language of the church but in simple words; it
was a stark prayer of one thought, "courage."
There was no bargaining, no promise to lead a
better life if my desire was granted. I wanted
courage—outward and inward courage. I didn't

ask for love or patience—just courage. Over and over again I prayed, "God, give me courage to hold my head high. Give me a singing soul." In some dim way I seemed to feel that if I were given these two gifts I could follow the cross, and in a far-off future would see its light.

My night nurse knew that I was awake, for several times she had given me a cigarette. At last she asked me if I had ever heard of miracles. She spoke gently of miracles she had seen, and of others which she believed. I listened. These were physical miracles. I felt that I had glimpsed a greater truth.

During the remainder of my stay in the hospital there was much to occupy my mind. I clung to the idea of courage and realized that its development depended on practice. It was not necessary to wait for some great occasion to display fortitude, but I must take advantage of every little opportunity. These cropped up in increasing numbers and seemed never-ending.

I began the practice of courage. I began to practice it in a very small way, so small that it may sound silly, but it was my way. I began first in the hospital and later at home where I had to lie on a couch all day, being too weak to sit up. I couldn't do anything by myself, not even walk without the support of my husband and nurse.

But I could think, and I knew what I wanted. It wasn't enough to speak cheerfully and not whine. I couldn't lighten my husband's burden, but I could keep it from growing heavier. My face was covered with a bandage from the hairline to the tip of my nose. This decoration was worn for three years. My eyelids had been slit at the corners to relieve the pressure on the eyeballs. At the height of the swelling, eyebrows as well as lids were lost in puffed flesh. Gradually the swelling subsided but a vaseline bandage had to protect the eyeballs from air. One eye had subsided to its normal size at the end of three years, but the other took ten months more. After Dr. Wheeler operated on the eyelids, I could close them and my face could be free from the bandage; that was three years later. While I wore it, only my mouth and chin were visible. If my lips should wear a bitter expression, cheerful words would lose their value! I must learn to smile. This was the first step on the road to courage.

The smile didn't stick long during the early days and weeks. I would feel my mouth drooping at the corners and would say, "Smile, darn you, smile." The resulting grimace would last only a split second, but I persevered, hour after hour, all day and at night too, when I was awake. The smile was only on the surface and I didn't realize until later that it had become an inward one. The discovery came in answer to a friend's question as to why there were no lines of bitterness around my mouth. "Because I don't feel bitter," I said, and recognized that the statement was true.

One day shortly after lunch, Dr. Bretz came to the hospital. It was an unusual hour for his visit and his coming was a delightful surprise. An extra surprise was the news he brought—my immediate removal to a furnished apartment.

I was tremendously pleased, for even a four-months' stay in a hospital where everyone, from doctors to chef, had been nice to me, couldn't overcome my original dislike. It was an odd experience to lie still and let other people make arrangements for me. It felt queer to be wrapped in a coarse, heavy blanket, to be lifted onto a litter and strapped there, to be carried out of the hospital and shoved into an ambulance. On arriving at the apartment house, the ambulance men carried the litter into an elevator and stood it upright against the wall. I then understood the reason for the straps.

"Don't be frightened, lady, you won't fall." The rough masculine voice had a kindly note.

I wasn't frightened; I was too weak to think about anything but the pain in my eyes. For

several weeks there had been no return of the
dreadful twisting stabs that had kept up for
months, but I was still apprehensive of a sudden
attack. A mere slide on a litter didn't worry me.
From the elevator through the foyer hall was
straight, but the entrance to a bedroom was a
different matter. There the litter became a seesaw,
and several times my feet were higher than my
head.

"Don't be frightened, lady," said the encouraging voice.

"Right," I whispered. "I know now just how
an armchair must feel when it is being wangled
through a narrow doorway."

I was lifted onto a bed and promptly fell asleep.
When I awoke the nurse brought me tea and sandwiches; after this light refreshment, I again slept.

I was forever falling asleep for the next few
months. Every morning after breakfast, the nurse
would bathe me. I hate being washed in patches;
I wanted to be put in a tub and get wet all at once,
and at my urgent insistence, after about a week,
this was done. Of course I had to be lifted in and
out of the tub, but my legs were growing stronger,
and with a towel wrapped around my body so
that my husband or the nurse could get a firm
grip, the helper would lift and I would push
with both hands on the tub rim, and my legs

would straighten up. The leg muscles were much
faster in recovering their strength than was the
rest of me. At first I had shuffled from bed to
couch supported by Dr. Bretz and the nurse,
but quite soon I could manage with only one
person. My spine didn't do so well, and it was six
months before I could sit up without support.

Those months were spent on the couch, eating
six times a day, thinking and falling asleep
before the thought amounted to much.

Once after an Episcopal priest had brought the
Sacrament and celebrated the short service for the
sick, I lay among the pillows while the words
"miserable sinner" rattled in my brain. The syllables made a pleasant rhythm—"miserable sinner
. . . miserable sinner . . . " Then a thought
came: "I am a child of God. Perhaps he doesn't
like his child to call herself a miserable sinner.
Perhaps our Heavenly Father would prefer to
hear about my virtues." I tried to find some, and
woke myself with a laugh. I didn't have one
single virtue that wasn't the result of education
and of environment. I've never been smugly
pious since.

Dr. Bretz always came home for luncheon to
break the monotony of my day; before leaving
he would read a magazine story. After dinner he
would read the newspaper and a crossword

puzzle. One evening a puzzle question was the name of the patron saint of shoemakers, and the word worked itself out as Crispin. The name caught my fancy, and while the Doctor was finishing the puzzle a legend grew in my mind. It was a pretty story, and I was just as surprised as my husband when I told it to him. Then other stories kept coming exactly as though I were reading them, and my husband was so interested that he had me recite them to a typist. That was quite an occupation during the day, and my husband was glad that I had found something to do.

Chapter 3

The inner life plays a more important part with the blind than it does with those who can see. Our thoughts can't be changed or our minds distracted by new sights or scenery. We can't even look out of the window and watch the passers-by if we feel lonely. This aloneness, this removal from the world, was one of my early discoveries.

During the five months following my return home from the hospital, there was nothing for me to do but lie on the couch and think. Among these thoughts were tentative plans for the coming days. Days—I didn't dare contemplate years —and plans had to be tentative because the world of the blind was to me an unknown place. As strength returned, I began to think about books. Making up stories was all very well, but I was hungry for books, and that hunger was not satisfied even by Dr. Bretz' reading detective stories to me every evening. He would read until midnight and then make coffee. He would bring the cups of coffee and a plate of cakes into the living room, and we would sip and nibble, discuss the book, and try to guess the villain of the plot. When we wanted second or third cups of coffee, my husband would refill the cups in the kitchen. The idea of a tray did not occur to him, nor did I suggest one, because a man's inefficiency about a house is amusing.

My husband wasn't the only one who read to me. Every Monday morning Father Hastings came to our apartment and after officiating as priest would read for several hours. He brought charming whimsical books from his own collection and sometimes the current issue of the *Atlantic* or *Harper's*. It was a long, long wait from Monday to Monday, and the hours of the day were long.

Intellectual freedom is the only freedom I have today, for blindness has destroyed my physical freedom. I realized this when I lay upon my couch, too weak to walk unless supported. My strength would come back. Eventually I would learn to move slowly about the room, but never again would it be possible for me to leave the house alone, never again to walk swiftly, to swing along by myself. No more traveling, except in books. It is not surprising, all things considered, that as soon as I was strong enough to sit up on the couch, unsupported by pillows, I began the study of Braille.

Braille, I knew, meant books that blind people read. Other than this, I hadn't the foggiest notion what Braille was or how it was read, but if other blind people learned it, so could I. Perhaps at that instant the Fate which had been hammering me took a nap, and Luck came to aid me in the form of a teacher, Theresa De Francis. Miss De Francis was not only an excellent instructor, but was gifted with a most pleasant personality and an understanding of my needs. She presented me with a primer and taught me the first ten letters of the alphabet.

The whole system of Braille, which was invented by the blind Frenchman, Louis Braille, resolves itself into a matter of simple mathematics. There are two columns of three raised dots each; the left is numbered down 1,2,3; the right, 4,5,6. Beginning with number 1 and combining it with each of the other dots, there are five combinations. Beginning with number 2, four more such combinations are obtained, and so on. When all possible two-dot combinations are exhausted, there are the combinations of three and four and five. I have never figured out exactly how many can be made, but there are so many more than are needed for the alphabet and punctuation marks that the remainder are used for syllables and whole words. Such signs, called contractions, simplify reading and make books shorter.

Numbers are formed by the first nine letters of the alphabet, the tenth being the zero.

Learning to read Braille is chiefly practice backed up by desire, and unless there is something physically wrong with the finger tips, such as lack of sensitiveness, learning is easy.

It took me one hour to learn to feel the little groups of dots that make up the first ten letters of the alphabet and to approximate the distance between them. A raised dot is a pesky thing, and the harder I pressed the less could I distinguish the difference between a single dot and two or three close together. I practised reading those ten letters and their unalphabetical arrangement on the rest of the page for a whole week. Hours flew swiftly, the tip of one forefinger grew sore, but by the end of the week I knew those letters. The following week I learned the next ten letters and rehearsed the preceding ten. In fourteen days twenty letters were mine, and the next week the alphabet was mastered, as well as groups of dots that symbolized words in common use. Here was something definite that I had worked for and earned for myself! It was extraordinarily gratifying.

The first Braille I learned had few contractions, and when I wanted to read English books, I got a key from the library. The key gave the contraction and its meaning. It was no more difficult to understand than a dictionary or a telephone directory, so that, after examining it, I boldly started with a volume of Milne's essays. The trick was never to slide over a contraction but to make sure of its meaning before going on. In the first essay, Milne describes taking a house in London where the garden was covered with "grkdsel." The combination of letters conveyed no idea to me; I tackled the key and words commencing with *g*, then *r*, then *k*, stuck at that word for an hour, and found that *k* placed cheek by jowl with another letter stood for "oun." The word was "groundsel," our old friend plantain! The *k* combination was mine from that moment. It occurs in many words.

America and England have now arrived at a standard Braille, and, although most hand-copied books remain in the simpler form, I won't bother to read them, because contractions shorten the books.

My incentive to learn to read was a driving force, my time unlimited. No longer were the twenty-four hours divided into day and night—any hour was suitable for study.

Books are supplied by the public library. And right here I'd like to pass on the information that the public library is a "rock in a weary land." It sends us free books, and we return them postage free. It is a marvelous service and a continuous pleasure. A Braille book review publishes monthly a list of new books with a few descriptive words. The contracted Braille known as grade two I conquered by the key with a high sense of accomplishment. Some years later I applied this method in learning to read French Braille. From the very first moment, I have enjoyed Braille. It gave me something to do, something to win for myself—and it's mine, my very own, a precious possession. I am never without books, essays, mystery stories, travel, biographies, fiction of all types, and many magazines. A Braille book has one special and charming asset: it can be read under the bedclothes on a cold night, and it is not necessary to remember to turn off the light before falling asleep.

In those first months of blindness, reading filled many hours which would otherwise have been vacant. Via a book, I could be in Africa, in Russia, in Paris, or in an English village. And when I paused in the reading, I was not brought back to the living room by a sight of its furniture.

No. I could remain indefinitely in the country about which I happened to be reading.

This curious phenomenon of blindness can also create confusion, for if I've been climbing a mountain or walking in a garden (in the book) it becomes difficult to walk across an actual rug, because, since I am not able to see, there is nothing that will bring me to the reality of my room. It is different with a person who can see. When he leaves off reading a book, no matter how vivid the impressions received may have been, the minute he turns his eyes away from the page, he is recalled to reality by the sight of familiar surroundings.

This inability quickly to return to reality restrained me from reading unpleasant books. Although I like mystery stories, the crime had to be committed before the book opened, or on the first page, because I wanted no description of cruelty.

When I could see, I could read almost any novel at a sitting. Now that I was blind, I found very few books worth the strain of continuous reading, the labor required by touch, and the spending of every available hour during successive days and nights. My reading finger would ache and grow stiff, and I would have to pause to give it a quick massage. Sometimes the ache traveled up my arm and danced a clog on my shoulder. To relieve the pain I would have to shift my position frequently.

Skipping in a Braille book is not so easy as in print. Consider the physique of a Braille book. A page is about eleven and a quarter inches long and ten and a half wide, and carries some 200 words—a little more than half the words on a page in a printed book. The paper is the thickness of strong wrapping paper, and, I'm told, is of light tan color. The embossed dots are not colored, although I always "see" them as black, like printed letters, which is absurd, of course. The book covers are heavy cardboard, covered with linen, and the backs are buckram. They are stout books, two or three inches thick, and it takes from three to six of them to reproduce an ordinary novel. Lincoln Steffen's "Autobiography" in Braille is in ten volumes.

Therefore, with many volumes to a book and a few words to a page, a stupid book would take a long time to read, although the poorly written book is not a complete loss. There is the manual occupation of reading, and the ticklish business of skipping a dull paragraph which may take a page or more. In skipping, I would turn a few leaves, feel a sentence, find the act still on, and turn some more. Maybe six or seven pages on I would discover that the words I was reading referred to something new, and then I had to turn back to pick up the context. However, even this effort was better than wading through much slush.

Blind people who don't read Braille miss a lot of fun. Books and friends take us away from our own thoughts and lighten the burden on our minds. We may be seeking information or entertainment, but in either case we find escape from ourselves.

I didn't find all Braille books interesting reading and tried Braille magazines as well. *The Reader's Digest* is outstanding, the Braille edition being the same as the printed, and really means more to the blind than to ordinary people.

The other Braille magazines, however, whether published in America or in England, are in a class by themselves. There is nothing like them in print. My knowledge of them grew from going through single copies, and there may have been a few issues that were better than those I read, but, if so, these escaped my observation.

The French magazines, among which are *Le Courier Musical et Literair* and *Les Propos du Mois*, are delightful. They contain well-written criticisms of the theater, concerts, and books. *Les*

Propos du Mois also actually gives pages from books, and articles by well-known authors from other magazines.

Poetry, after blindness, was lost to me, with many other things. Looking at a poem, one sees its pattern at a glance, blank verse, the vision and length of the verses, their rhyme or rhythm. In Braille there can be no such bird's-eye view, and in feeling letters and words, an accent may be altered which alters the beat. If I had had the habit of memorizing poetry, it might have been different, but just reading it was most unsatisfactory.

Word sounds have come to mean more to me now than formerly. In reading Braille, I must mentally pronounce each word as I read it, syllable by syllable, until I have it all. There is a sound and savor, irrespective of meaning. A word may have the vibrant tone of an open *D* string on a cello, or give a piquant touch, like saffron, to a sentence. And there are ugly words that may be poignant, as when Lady Ashley, in Hemingway's "The Sun Also Rises," can only cry out her sacrifice and heartbreak in the crass vulgarity of her social set.

Books in Braille have proved to be a continual experiment. When I began to read, the books were rather disappointing. I had read the well-known authors in print, and so tried the lesser lights. It soon became evident why they were lesser. Later, however, with books being so generously and rapidly supplied by the government, I made another discovery—that Braille is a severe test of an author's style.

The enforced slower pace of reading by touch instead of at a glance, the finger feeling each word, and frequently each letter of a word, permits no author's carelessness to escape. The hackneyed phrase, the trite expression, or the too-frequent use of such words as "beautiful," "wonderful," "startling," and so forth, register a black mark against the writer. I was a rapid sight reader, although not so rapid as to compete with the page-at-a-glance performer. Referring now only to modern fiction, I could read a hundred pages in an hour. Such a book read aloud to me is at the rate of forty-five pages an hour. I've been told that the average rate of a blind reader is fifty to a hundred words a minute. This, of course, is not reading aloud. I haven't tried being timed in fiction, but was timed with Deems Taylor's "Of Men and Music," which, while not in the least heavy, still is not so light as a gay novel. I managed forty-three words to the minute. However, with Leslie Ford's "Ill-met by Moon-light," a swift detective story, I read seventy-three words a minute. When I remember that an ordinary printed page contains about three hundred and fifty words, I jump a mathematical hurdle and say that it takes me ten times as long to read a book in Braille as it did in print. This slow reading also awards delightful prizes in the choice of an unusual word, or a surprise ending to a sentence. Do the authors ever hear the chuckles, or feel the happy thoughts that are sent through the open windows of my living room? If they do, then the slovenly writers might feel a slap on the wrist. Perhaps the living-room windows had better be kept closed.

It might be a good idea to talk about the nice books when the windows are open, and begin now with the dull books. My first disappointment was Galsworthy.

Galsworthy had been to me one of the good English writers. I had enjoyed his Forsyte Saga and, when Forsyte descendants were carried on and the trilogy, "Maid in Waiting," "Ah Wilderness," and "One More River," was put in Braille, I welcomed it enthusiastically. Each printed volume made three large volumes in Braille, and I anticipated several weeks of pleasant reading. To my disappointment and surprise, Galsworthy proved to be a careless and repetitive writer who could not stand the test of

Braille. If he had always written in this slipshod manner, it had escaped me in my former rapid reading. There could be no such escape in Braille. A most noticeable, dull repetition was found in the conversation. Every character was described, and frequently, as assenting thus: " 'Yes,' she said and nodded" or " 'Yes,' he said and nodded." When in the very beginning of the seventh Braille volume appeared, " 'Yes,' Claire said and nodded," I yipped.

A Galsworthy contemporary, Walpole, proved equally disappointing. Slipshod workmanship rather than a small vocabulary must account for the frequency with which he used the word "wonderful."

There are many other defects, such as muddled style, poor plot, or wrong statements, that become particularly noticeable in slow reading. A printed book may be good, bad, or mediocre. In Braille, which is an embossed version of print, there is no halfway. Feeling of each word emphasizes bad points as well as good, and an author falls into one of the two extremes. Among the millions of printed books a great majority is worthless, and Braille doesn't change the proportion. Still, books play as important a part in my life as they have always done, and I frequently have the pleasure of coming upon a book that stands up well under the test which Braille imposes on it.

I encountered a good detective story not long ago, "As Simple as Poison." It wasn't the plot that fascinated me, but the gaiety of the telling. It is almost impossible to create a gay atmosphere in Braille, so that this book is to the author's credit.

Knowing what Braille can do to an author's work, I am doubly pleased to find one book that stands the test. This book is James Boyd's "Roll River," which I read several years ago. It remains in my memory as an outstanding example of what a good book can be. The plot unfolded in a unique way, the style was delightful, there was a delectable choice of colorful words; the characters were so alive that when I closed the last volume I felt as though I were saying good-by to lifelong friends. I had lived with them continuously, for my reading was interrupted only by daily duties and visiting friends. To me there has never been any other book quite like it. I forgot my stiff finger, aching arm, and throbbing shoulder, and remember the familiar streets of a town on the bank of a river and a group of pleasant people.

When a book can take me from my daily life and transplant me into new surroundings, it is

more than a book. "Roll River" was an experience. I am unacquainted with its author. In fact,
none of the authors mentioned is personally
known to me, and my opinion is an expression of
the effect their writings have on me as a Braille
reader. A commonplace style makes easy reading in Braille because the next word can be
anticipated. It is like turning a printed page
and knowing what the first word on the
following page will be. An unusual style slows
reading.

When Noel Coward's "Present Indicative"
was sent to me from the library, it didn't excite
my curiosity for I knew little about the author
except that he was an actor and a playwright.
Its title was clever. I opened the book lazily and
had my attention caught by the first paragraph.
If I hadn't continued reading, I would have
missed many chuckles at the surprise endings of
sentences. Here is one: "He had a superior manner, but then his position as organist of the
Royal Chapel brought him in contact with
members of the Royal Family as well as with
The—Almighty." The pause is mine to indicate
the perceptible instant it took to read the word.
When its meaning was grasped, my laugh was
spontaneous.

This line lives up to one of Max Eastman's definitions of a joke, in his "Enjoyment of Laughter." The surprise ending comes with great force in Braille. A finger can't take in a sentence at a glance; the last word comes *bang*, and the period becomes a laugh.

Chapter 4

It was three months after I returned home from the hospital before I was able to sit up at the dining table, and, when I did, I found that I had to sit in an armchair, not for support, but because of a strange new fear. Sitting in a straight chair, the space about me seemed so vast that I was terrorized by the thought that an unwary movement might plunge me headlong into it. My horror was reminiscent of the Thing that had crouched on my hospital bed. I had to fight hard to conquer that fear—the fear of the unseeable.

My plan of campaign was simple. I chose a light cane-bottomed chair, and had it placed a step from my bed. This was the Field of Combat. Every morning I'd screw my courage to a sticking point, take the one step, and sit on the chair for a minute. Well, perhaps it wasn't a full sixty-second minute—in fact, I'm quite sure it wasn't for many, many days.

There were mornings when it was difficult to make the courage stick, other mornings when the one step became a series of toddles. Finally I reached the stage where I sat on the chair and counted sixty. But the numbers had a way of scurrying that was not wholly honest. When I discovered this trick, I began forcing myself to sit still after saying "sixty," and the figures gave up their skipping habits. Yet even after learning to sit on this particular chair for a little while, I still found myself afraid of strange chairs, and to sit in one required an effort. The struggle lasted for nearly two years and ended in a complete victory for my side.

In this early period of readjustment I was amazed and, strange as it may sound, intensely interested in learning to perform silly little everyday actions in a new way. Nor was it just learning something new. Quite the contrary: it was learning to do the old thing in a new way, and simultaneously learning to forget the former method. No longer could I nonchalantly squeeze toothpaste on a brush. I tried that, and the paste landed anywhere but on the bristles. I used to think that a toothbrush consisted of bristles and a handle. I was wrong. True, a toothbrush does possess these two parts, but it also has a back, two sides, and two ends, with many spots in between. To be able to hit the right spot, I worked out the system of running my thumb along the handle until it reached the bristles, then, keeping it there, I squeezed the tube. Most of the paste spreads on the bristles, with a small gob on my thumbnail.

Another lesson I had to learn was to walk around a room alone. Without a friendly hand to guide me, my usual swinging step brought my forward foot into sharp contact with a piece of furniture, and the result was a bruised instep, ankle, or shin. My step had to be shortened and my feet raised only high enough to skim the rug. Unhappily, I still don't always remember these things, and so keep a permanent collection of black-and-blue spots.

Except for reading Braille, there was little I could do at this time, but I did make a few small advances. For one thing, I began dressing for dinner, which pleased my husband very much. Until then I had worn hostess gowns made of a silk crepe that didn't crush. The gowns were in light colors, of a simple style, with round neck and angel sleeves of chiffon to match the crepe, and were fairly easy to get into. I would feel the neckline to discover the front, then put my right arm through the right armhole, my left hand holding the compress, which I was still obliged to wear, in place across my eyes, while my right hand pulled the neck up over my right ear and rested on my head. At this point, my hands shifted on the compress, my left hand went through the proper armhole, the neckline fell into place, and both hands pulled the dress down and tied its string belt.

A dress with tight sleeves and smaller armholes presented difficulties, but my system remained the same. I just had to be more careful, and not try to yank the dress over my head.

A real dress helped my morale. We began to have friends to dinner, and when we played auction afterward, a glimpse of my former life seemed to reappear.

Cards were quite an amusement, and could be managed. Dr. Bretz had an ordinary deck marked in Braille in the upper right-hand corner. I shuffled, dealt, and arranged my hand. My card memory had been trained since childhood, and was still with me, so that I never had to ask about a turned trick. The speed of the game was slowed, because each player had to name the card played, and I had to ask about dummy.

About this period, Miss De Francis taught me to thread a needle. There are special needles for the blind which have a notch at the top of the eye, through which a tightly drawn thread will slip. This was the kind I used. I never knew much about sewing and the few things I did know are of no value now. Years ago, the wife of Bishop Whittaker taught me to darn, and I practiced on the Bishop's socks. We had lived next door to the Bishop, and I was in their house a great deal. My mother had shown me how to hem table linen in the convent method, and I had also embroidered. Now these accomplishments were in the discard, and my needlework consisted in sewing a rip in a slip or nightgown. But even that was an achievement. In order that I might not sew a white garment with black thread or vice versa, I cut three notches in both ends of the spools of black thread, and left the white ones smooth. If I had a colored garment to mend I had to ask someone else to choose the right color. Colored threads were kept in a separate box, and when one was wanted it had to be found by someone with eyes. There is always a difference in materials and styles of dresses, and I had no difficulty in choosing the dress, having once been told its color.

The thing that gave me the greatest pleasure at this time was having guests at our dinner table. This was even nicer than going out to dinner, although we did that too. If our friends lived at a distance, we took a taxi, but if they lived within a few blocks, we walked.

Speaking of entertaining and being entertained at dinner brings up a whole new phase of the problem of readjustment. While I was still in bed, or confined to the couch, I fed myself propped up in bed with a tray on my lap, and it never occurred to me that when I would be able to sit at the dining table my former manners wouldn't work. The surprise came when, having graduated from sick table to dining table, I found myself confronted with a plate full of soup. Having been taught in my youth to turn the spoon away from me, I moved it in that direction, and it traveled across the plate until it reached the outer rim, its journey preceded by a soupy wave which went "blop" on the cloth.

My dismay was only temporary. I tried again, this time bringing the spoon toward me. The movement was novel, and a bit awkward, and the only discoverable difference in result was that the wave fell this time on my napkin.

I considered the situation carefully. I don't like soup. It's such a waste of space. But I had to know what to do with it when I encountered it. It was easier to turn the spoon away but to put my left hand on the outer rim of the plate would look awkward, so I finally adopted a system of resting my left forefinger lightly on the inner rim, bringing the spoon toward it, and pausing before reaching the spot where that finger rested.

In trying to figure out when my right hand approaches my left, and how I gauge the distance between them and yet cannot judge the distance to an inanimate object, I have come to the conclusion that I know where my left hand is; therefore, if I rest my left hand on an object as a guide, my right hand can find it. Oh, yes, I can manage soups now, if necessary.

Some desserts I found unmanageable, particularly huckleberry and custard pies, parfaits in tall narrow glasses, and sloppy puddings on flat plates. Spaghetti and noodles too proved unconquerable. I learned, through sad experience, to refuse all such treacherous items, and gave as my reason my desire to preserve my slender figure. It was a neat idea, but it didn't originate with me. Food traps possess amazing ingenuity, and the fun lies in outwitting them.

Forks, I found, were very tricky, and possessed peculiarities which I had never before suspected. In my own home, I could gauge a forkful of food by its weight, but dining out had its snares. At one house the end of the fork handle had a curve which was the reverse of any I had hitherto handled, and, as a result, on my first encounter I found myself trying to eat from the back of the prongs instead of from the front. I learned never to use a knife, because I couldn't measure the size of piece I was cutting; therefore my meat was, and is, always cut up for me.

Glasses I had always supposed to be upright creatures, but I soon discovered that with the slightest excuse or touch they took a malicious joy in falling prostrate. A highball glass once even poked me in the nose, disgusted, no doubt, at being filled with plain water. Its nasty temper took me off guard. I had thought it an ordinary tumbler, judging by its base, and failed to approximate the extra height. That experience taught me to feel a glass from base to rim before lifting it to my mouth. Stem glasses, especially fragile wine or cocktail glasses, offer great excitement. A goblet, even a thin one, is more solid. I gave considerable thought to the management of these glasses before trying to handle them, and have learned to outwit their trickery. Now, they stand without hitching, so to speak.

Avoiding stumbling blocks, I found, produced a divided mind at a dinner table and I felt a distinct sense of accomplishment when I finally learned to join in the conversation, nonchalantly tossing the ball of repartee with one part of my mind, while focusing intently with the other part on what my hands were doing. In all this,

I had to avoid the appearance of fumbling among the china and cutlery, to make my careful touch appear casual, in order that my blindness might not be too obvious.

I had been a smoker for years and blindness did not change my enjoyment. Learning to light my own cigarette was an achievement in itself. I did it by sliding a finger of my left hand from my mouth along the cigarette to the tip, then bringing up the match flame with my right hand until I felt the heat on the finger resting at the tip of the cigarette. I still scorch my fingers occasionally, but this trick is necessary in order to avoid the real danger of lighting a cigarette in the middle and having it burn both ways, throwing off a glowing tip on a dress or rug.

Walking is really an adventure, and my first attempts on the street taught me a number of things. My step had to be shortened because of unobservable depressions or rises in the sidewalk. My husband held me firmly by one arm and told me whether a gutter was three or seven inches high, which didn't do a bit of good. Apparently I couldn't judge inches except by sight. We crossed streets on the bias and I never negotiated the opposite gutter successfully.

All this procedure was wrong, but we were both ignorant of the proper method. And there is a proper method, which I later read in a Braille magazine. The rules are that the blind person should always hold the arm of his guide, instead of the reverse. This position allows the blind person to tighten his grasp at the indication of a stumble. The gesture becomes automatic. Always cross a street at right angles. I don't know why this is successful, but it is, and the gutter across the way is easy. I also found that a stick measures the height or depth of a gutter or step—it seems to guide my foot. A blind woman's stick can be a swagger stick, not a hooked cane. I have three rather nice ones, a black, a black-and-white, and a purple, to match my clothes. My sticks have to be made extra long, because I am tall and don't want to stoop at every gutter.

Gutters, I discovered, are not only unfriendly, they can be positively vicious. A gutter is a delusion, a snare, and a number of other things, all of which are unpleasant. I would not feel justified to write a character reference for a single gutter in New York City. Nor do I demand the impossible. The combination of curb and gutter may not be capable of a moral standard, but surely, surely a standard of uprightness could be forced upon it. But no, it will surreptitiously slip into the street or hump its shoulders, ready to sling a piece of concrete in my face. It crouches sulkily or springs up to catch my foot. The gutters in my neighborhood I have learned to know, and I recognize their individual idiosyncrasies.

Waverly Place at Fifth Avenue is a respectable street. It looks up the Avenue and, glancing over its shoulder, sees the Washington Arch and the Square. It remains respectable for a little way, until safely out of sight of the Avenue, then after crossing Sixth Avenue, it goes haywire. It actually splits and goes on both sides of the Northern Dispensary. It makes up its differences before risking the crossing of Seventh Avenue. Having lost its dignity and quarreled with itself, it can't cross the Avenue in an honest straight line, but dashes across diagonally. That is its last spurt. It will never be straight again. It weakly crawls to Bank Street and stops exhausted. The exhaustion is exemplified in the east gutter that whispers, "Excuse me, please. I didn't mean to be a gutter, I'm only a threshold."

The Fourth Street gutter stands high and powerful, and yells, "Who do you think you are?" The one at Bleeker Street cries, "Who're you stepping on?"

A curb doesn't like to be stepped on. It considers itself part of the gutter, and the sidewalks must take care of themselves. Their smoothness or unevenness is not its concern, and, turning its back on them, it ignores pavement trickery.

Pavement tricks are numerous. Uptown, where sidewalks are supposed to be well-mannered, they will remove a whole slab and present me with cinders to walk on. Once a Fifth Avenue pavement covered itself with a bridge and barred ramps that caught my heels. The artistic temperament of sidewalks finds a congenial habitat in Greenwich Village, where they continually hump and shrink and curl.

Chapter 5

Without being conscious of the fact, I ceased to count the hours in a day; weeks slipped by and sometimes the casual mention of a date would tell me that a month had passed. I was forming new habits, although they had not yet become automatic.

Morning began with a breakfast tray brought to my room an hour or two after Dr. Bretz had gone to his office. When I was dressed, our maid, who had been a hospital nurse during the war, would wash my eyes with a warm saline solution and put on a fresh compress. My husband never looked at those disfigured eyes. He preferred to remember my eyes as they had once been.

Much of the day was spent on the couch, but I had books to read. Dr. Bretz had gone over the library catalogue with me and had marked books which sounded interesting. He would also go to the public library and talk to Lucy A. Goldthwaite about them. Since I had been brought up on the classics, for new reading I had to choose little-known authors, many of whom should have been less known.

I talked over the stories with my husband, who was interested because I was. He really was pleased that his wife could make sense out of pages of jumbled dots. It was pleasant to be praised and very encouraging.

My reading was chiefly during the morning, for my husband continued to come home for luncheon and friends had begun to come in the afternoon. The maid would wheel the tea wagon in front of the couch and a guest would pour tea. Frequently there would be a little group of three or four and conversation would be gay. I would tell Arthur about these friends; it made a nice dinner topic. He would chuckle over some of the stories and I knew that his eyes were twinkling. I had loved to see the twinkle and I began to listen for its equivalent in his voice and to plan for it. It was surprising how many funny things could happen during the day and I hoarded them all.

My interest in planning meals revived. As I knew my husband's tastes, the task was easy. Then, too, he was always so appreciative of a surprise that even thinking of it gave me joy.

Our little table was jolly despite half my face being covered with a bandage.

The sight of that white patch with its hidden tragedy made my husband suffer terribly. He never complained, but I knew that he would gladly and willingly have taken my blindness if I could have been spared. There was nothing to be said or done. We could only cling together, each one pretending to be brave so as to encourage the other. To stand by helpless and know that a loved one is suffering is worse than physical pain and my blindness added a final touch of cruelty— I was unable to watch my husband's face when talking to him.

I had one sickening experience with this, and perhaps there were other occasions when I remained in ignorance.

A friend had taken me to New Jersey for a drive and I had called on two of our farm neighbors. On our return we found Arthur in the living room. I took the many-folded veil from across the compress, and sat down without bothering about my hat and coat because I was eager to tell the story.

I laughed and chattered about my call on the Hadels. I told how the older brother had helped me from the car and led me to the house; how the younger Hadel had come in and exclaimed, "You look as natural as ever, sitting there smoking." I told how at the Higgins, Mr. Higgins had led me across the grass, saying, "You always did like to walk on grass."

I didn't notice Arthur's silence because my words were tumbling out so fast, but when I paused my friend suggested that we go into the bedroom and take off our things. She closed the bedroom door and said in a low voice, "My dear, I couldn't make you stop talking. The tears were rolling down Arthur's face. He was holding back a sob with all his force. I was afraid he would break down."

He remembered me as dashing in to see the Hadels and running across the Higgins' lawn and he couldn't bear to picture me being carefully led.

I had enjoyed my trip and had thought that Arthur would love to hear all the details, and I had hurt him.

After that experience I gave expurgated versions of stories, allowed no hint of difficulties to creep in, and strove to convince him that living was as simple as it had been.

He was so afraid of my falling that he wouldn't let me walk alone. He would hold me firmly by one arm and the maid was instructed to take care of me while he was away. This idea didn't

coincide with my conception of self-reliance. I therefore practiced moving about the living room and then progressed into the hall leading to the bedrooms and bath. I did these things when he was out because my fumbling slowness would have grieved him. The exercise made me surer on my feet and steadier in all my movements. I didn't let Arthur see me try to walk alone until I could walk a few steps with comparative freedom. Then, one day, I got up from the couch and walked to the bathroom, lightly touching a piece of furniture, then the hall door. He was both surprised and pleased and a bit relieved, too, I think.

My husband and I had many cunning times together, as do all happily married couples— little incidents that in the aggregate make for close companionship, but that taken singly seem unimportant.

Arthur always greeted me the instant he came into the apartment, then he put away his coat and hat, cleaned up, and settled himself in a big chair with pipe or cigarette. One evening, after a pipe was filled, he asked, "What have you been doing with yourself all afternoon?"

"A man came to tea and read love poems to me."

"What's this? What's this?"

There were the sounds of a match being struck, a puff-puff of a pipe, and his body relaxing in the chair.

"Who's the fellow who read love poems to my wife? Tell me his name and I'll punch his head for him."

"Jim," I gurgled. "From Tennyson back to Herrick, with stops at all wayside stands."

The Doctor chuckled, "I admire his taste. Did he declaim in his best sermon manner?"

"Not at all. He read very well. He didn't singsong the verses and he didn't turn a poem into a paragraph. I hate poetry read like prose. Jim made an infinitesimal pause at the end of each line so it was easy to follow the rhythm and rhyme."

"I suppose you complimented him on his reading."

"Of course I did."

"You are leading the cloth astray, and you don't even stick to one church."

"Pause in your denunciation. You know that you don't like people to talk operations to you. Well, don't you suppose that a minister, priest, or deacon may find it a relief to have a hostess who doesn't talk dogma, or doesn't want the temperature of her soul taken?"

"You are a wicked woman. How about a cocktail before dinner?"

This was a pleasant way of not answering my question. It was nice to hear Arthur chuckle. He had been under a long, terrific strain and must continue to be, so that I cherished every spark of gaiety.

He played the piano a bit and one Sunday afternoon improvised a sentimental melody to which I recited a saccharine verse. We sang it over and over again and laughed until we were weak. My son came in during the performance and joined in the fun. Our neighbors may have wondered if we were crazy but we never gave them a thought. Whether or not Arthur joked to keep up my spirit, or I laughed to encourage him, I don't know, but our teamwork was excellent. More and more friends came to our house and no reference was ever made to my blindness. We all acted as though there were nothing the matter with me.

Life became a game in which my hand held no trumps and I knew it, but I didn't throw my cards on the table. I stuck it out.

When friends were with me in the afternoon, I openly spoke of blindness but never in Arthur's presence because any reference to it hurt him. A few of our intimate friends were tremendously interested in the little things I did by myself. They seemed to find something miraculous about my lighting a cigarette, walking a few steps guided by one hand touching the furniture, and so on. The word "wonderful" soon became a bore. I didn't guess how often it would be thrust upon me in the future. In the beginning I used to protest and patiently explain how I did things, only to discover that people didn't want to have their illusions debunked, they preferred to have a wonder-working friend. It's a curious point of view. My husband's attitude was much better in this regard. He apparently took it for granted that as my strength had returned, so too had my ability to do things.

In the spring, two years after being brought home from the hospital, my strength was so well established that Dr. Bretz felt that it was safe to leave me with the maid. He went to our farm for a few days and came back with a mass of plum blossoms and daffodils. He arranged the flowers in vases, although he didn't know anything about fixing flowers, and led me around the room to feel them. I cherish this memory. The next day, a Monday, he said that he didn't feel well enough to go to his office, and stayed in bed. On Tuesday morning, at nine o'clock, our maid woke me and said that the doctor was lying on the living-room couch and that she thought he wasn't well. She put a negligee on me and led me to the living room. I sat in a chair across the room from the couch on which my husband lay. I didn't speak to him or touch him for fear of disturbing his sleep. I asked the maid what seemed to be the matter, and she said that she would call the elevator operator.

While she telephoned the switchboard, I sat in the quiet stillness. The earthy fragrance of daffodils seemed to touch my face. My husband slept quietly, a restful sleep that would refresh him.

The elevator girl came in, stood for a moment, and then said softly, "Don't be frightened, Mrs. Bretz. I'll call the superintendent." She hurried away, without closing the door.

I turned to the maid and asked steadily, "Is the doctor dead?"

"Yes, Mrs. Bretz." There was a catch in her voice.

For a second time I had been forced to hear a bitter truth.

The superintendent came and offered expressions of sympathy. There followed a doctor from St. Vincent's Hospital, who after a cursory examination said that my husband had been dead six hours. The maid suggested that I dress, and, while we were in my bedroom, two policemen came. I finished dressing and went back into the living room. I suppose that my bandaged face and Dr. Bretz's quiet position reassured them, for one telephoned to the Charles Street Station and said that it wasn't necessary for two of them to stay and that he would make a report. I offered the remaining policeman coffee, which he refused, saying that he never drank it. I talked with him a little, and found him most polite. I instructed the maid to tell the switchboard operator to telephone my son and my brother, and gave her the numbers. My son arrived shortly before the policeman left. There was no one to direct things but myself. Many things depended on me, and I had to be steady. I had to tell my son of the people to be notified, I had to order meals, and I had to keep myself from being a bother—to stay put in a chair and not be waited on. My son had placed a screen around the couch because my husband must not be moved until after the medical examiner had been there.

The medical examiner came at three o'clock. He asked more questions about my eyes than about Dr. Bretz.

At that time blindness proved to be something of a blessing. My last memory of my husband was when his blue eyes had twinkled at a funny story I had told him. And that is the way I think of him. And because his last gift of flowers was on the fifteenth of April, since then, on that date, I buy flowers for myself—but never daffodils.

Another living memory is of a time when I went away for a short visit. Before leaving, I remarked to my husband that he would have a rest, and not have to think of me. He said, "I am always thinking of you." A year after his death, I was lying on the couch, half asleep, when I was awakened by the sound of a key in the door. "Arthur," I exclaimed, and sat up. My son came in. The fact that I called my husband's name showed me that, subconsciously, I too was always thinking of him. His key in the door had meant a gay little jump of my heart. I used to begin to listen for him at half after five, and even now I get restless at that hour and find myself listening for the sound that will never come again.

I may be alone, but I am not lonely. I am happy for my husband, and that makes it impossible to be unhappy for myself. There are pleasant things to think of—and there is meditation.

Chapter 6

When my husband's estate was settled, I bought a small apartment in a cooperative house. I had visited friends in the house during the years when I could see and knew its floor plans.

My apartment consists of a living room, one bedroom, kitchen, and bath. There is no servant's room, so I hired a maid by the day. She came in the morning and stayed until after dinner. The new home was quickly settled but it took me a long time to become familiar with it. The daily routine presented no particular difficulties. The maid was efficient and pleasant. All I had to do was to concentrate on myself and to endeavor to find the courage to go on alone. There was no incentive for smiles or gaiety, no one whose coming brought me joy.

I went down deep within myself and fought it out. I was still alive—would have to go on living—and I wouldn't be a quitter. I'd take it on the chin, but my chin should be up.

I approached life from a different angle, perhaps a selfish one. The fact that stared me in the face was that I had to live with myself. Therefore, I must make myself a companion I could live with. This may sound involved, but I was in deadly earnest. I couldn't stand living with a whiner or a grouch, that was definite. All right then, I must smile and again find a song in my heart. While in one sense this was difficult, in another it was not, because I knew the way, having traveled it before.

I picked up the strands of my old life and wove a new pattern. I invited people to tea and to dinner. Tea parties were a success; dinners were not. My first experience with a dinner party taught me that I couldn't know when my guests were ready for a next course, whether or not a subject of conversation was exhausted or if a guest had something more to contribute. No, as a dinner hostess I was a failure. I tried it several times and always had the uneasy sense of falling down on the job, so gave up that form of entertainment.

After a few months I began to consider more practical matters. I was living on capital and could figure out how long it would last at the rate at which it was being spent. The x was, how long would my life last. America was in the midst of the depression and the answer to my problem was obvious. Expenses must be cut. I dismissed the maid.

I was perfectly well and strong and it never occurred to me that it wouldn't be easy to take care of myself and the apartment. I had accepted blindness and thought myself cognizant of its limitations. Well, I wasn't. In every picayune daily action, blindness lurked to trip me up. It was amazing and it was constant. I didn't get mad, but I did get fiercely determined to win the fight or go down with flag flying.

My friends were horrified at my decision to live alone.

"You can't do it; it's impossible."

"You can't do it; there might be an accident."

"You can't do it; suppose the house caught fire."

And so it went with the refrain "You can't."

Each protest I answered with, "I don't know what I can do until I try. I only know that there is a greater chance of happiness for me living alone than boarding with uncongenial people. Please don't worry about me. I can be murdered only once and a fire might occur wherever I live."

The morning of the new adventure had come. There was no maid to prepare breakfast—but what of that? I had frequently made coffee. I went into the kitchen, not with a bold and determined step, however, because my feet don't work that way while guided by a feeling hand. I touched the table, the sink, and the edge of the stove and came to shelves. My fingers moved lightly among pots, pans, jars, and crockery. Minutes passed while I felt through them a second and a third time, but found no coffeepot. Suddenly I recalled that the maid had said that she would put the coffeepot and teapot on the stove with the electric plate. Sure enough, there they were as cozy as you please. I took the cover off the coffeepot and examined the percolator. The spot in my brain that mechanical sense should occupy, bears the sign "Vacant." Reluctantly I put the coffeepot aside and filled the enamel teapot with water. When the water boiled I sloshed a teaball in it.

While I was waiting for the water in the teapot to boil, I had brought out a loaf of bread and had cut a slice; the slice started nice and thin and ended in a wide wedge. The chunk was unfit for toast, nor could it be conveniently broken into small pieces for buttering. Oh, well, toast wasn't really necessary with tea; buttered Uneeda biscuits would do. If I had been an emphatic person, that meal would have been called a "hell-of-a-breakfast."

For three mornings that menu was repeated, until a man visitor explained the workings of the coffeepot. During those days I had asked two women, and each one had said, after looking at the pot, "It isn't like mine. I don't know how it works." It takes a man!

Once having grasped the principle of the percolator, I made coffee. After measuring the coffee and water with the precision of a chemist filling a prescription, I would place the percolator on an electric plate. Electricity is slower than gas, but much safer for me. When the coffeepot was firmly placed, I would get the butter from the icebox so that it would have a chance to soften. Then I would go into the living room, smoke a cigarette, and think over plans for the day. At first, my coffee was quite poor, as I could not gauge the time for percolating, but eventually I learned to sniff it. A nose is a valuable assistant.

The toast problem was solved for me when I discovered that I could purchase bread already sliced. My system was this: when the fragrance of coffee trotted into my nose, I would go to the kitchen, put the pot in the sink, and place a flat five-and-ten-cent-store toaster on the electric plate. Then I would put a piece of bread on the toaster, place a cup in the sink, and pour the coffee. This was so that, in case the cup ran over, it would not make a mess.

After the coffee-pouring ritual, and when I thought enough time had elapsed for the toast to be done, I was ready to eat. The first piece of toast is never so good as the following two, because I have invented a system of timing. When the first slice is buttered and half eaten, it is the moment for turning the bread on the toaster, and when the first slice is finished, the second is ready. This, of course, is if I keep my mind on what I am about. If day dreaming takes possession of me, the toast burns.

After breakfast, my routine was to take a tub and dress. I shall never forget my first tub bath alone, when I found myself with a washcloth in one hand and a cake of soap in the other—and the soap got away from me. On the spur of the moment, I had to invent a technique for dealing with such a situation. I stuck one knee up out of the water, and draped the washcloth on it. That would be safe at any rate. Then I gently pursued the cake of soap with both hands, while it dodged round corners and hid in areaways. I finally captured it.

After bathing and dressing, I washed my breakfast dishes. This I accomplished by first putting everything in the sink. There weren't many dishes, of course—there never are—a plate, a cup and saucer, a few pieces of silver, and the teapot or coffeepot. I picked up one piece at a time, holding it firmly in my left hand, and never letting go until it was washed and dried and put away.

On that first morning after breakfast, the next household chore I attempted was bedmaking. I had left the bed to air when I got up, and now approached it with determination and considerable misgiving. I grasped a sheet firmly in my outstretched hands and waved it wildly in what I hoped was the right direction. It wasn't. I tried a second and more cautious wave, without much greater success. But I stuck with it, and finally worked out my system. Making a bed my way resembles a walking tour. The first sheet is waved, or rather rippled, across the bed. Then both hands smooth it, inch by inch, pulling edges back and forth to get out the wrinkles. Kneeling on a bed to straighten the sheet on the opposite side from where I stood didn't prove successful, and I found it was much better to walk around the bed and perform all operations from the point of greatest vantage.

Next the living room had to be dusted, and on this occasion I learned one of my most valuable lessons. Dusting a table with the cloth held in my right hand sent a vase of flowers crashing to the floor. Finding the vase and each stem, and wiping up the water, which meant getting down on hands and knees and keeping my head bent low so as not to bump my face against a table leg or near-by chair, taught me always to move my left hand gently and slowly in front of my right, which held the cloth. In this way, small objects, such as ash trays and papers of matches, could be detected and picked up before the duster caught them and swept them to the floor.

Another thing I learned from that first morning was that it would be a great saving in money, time, and nerves if breakable items were gradually eliminated from the room. Now in my living room there are no breakable ornaments.

The white marble mantel holds five brass candlesticks, an old French hand lamp, and several ash trays. All are in brass and match the andirons and fire hood. On the tea wagon, at one end of the room, stands a copper samovar, with an ash tray, and on the shelf underneath a tray holds a silver cocktail shaker and jigger. On a long table in one corner there are a lamp, a pewter tankard, and a liqueur set which is kept closed. A small bookcase holds the radio and Braille books; another table is for the telephone. On top of the piano there are a pair of mahogany candlesticks and several pieces of copper. If in the process of dusting the furniture any of these things bounces on the floor, it does not break.

Vases of flowers are kept on the window shelf beside my chair and, if there are too many for this space, I use fat pottery jars that are not easily upset.

My love of flowers surprises people. They thought that it was the fragrance, and in the early years of my blindness gave me roses, violets, and lilies, and in the spring hyacinths, freesias, and narcissi. Then one autumn a great longing for chrysanthemums overwhelmed me and I bought a bunch. The woodsy odor brought a vision of trees in vivid colors, the box hedge trimmed with dew-spangled cobwebs, brilliant sunshine and a sapphire sky, a tang of frost in the air that gave a zest for life. A jar of chrysanthemums on the window ledge and dreams.

I've experimented with other flowers such as asters, gladioli, anemones, and so on. I pat their heads and touch their leaves. They are not just flowers in a vase or bowl; they're memories of a garden.

The blossoms on the window ledge are near my chair. All the furniture must be placed near the walls to keep the center of the room clear, so that I can get around without bumps or the danger of a fall.

The easiest solution to floor cleaning, I found, was to let it alone, for I discovered from the remarks of candid friends that I could never be sure of having caught every scrap of paper or bit of thread with the carpet sweeper, or of having achieved a consistently good polish on every part of the hardwood border. So now I leave the floors for the man who comes once a week to do all the jobs which I feel incapable of handling alone.

That first day alone in my small apartment was one of many trials. But the next day was not quite so difficult, and the next was a tiny bit easier than the preceding one. And so, in time, I struggled through to a fairly smooth-working routine, which is still in effect.

The morning follows fairly closely the order already outlined. Before luncheon, which is usually a sandwich and canned fruit, I telephone the grocer for the day's supplies. Most of the food which I prepare for myself at home comes out of cans. They are easy to open, while jars possess obstreperous characteristics and devilish ingenuity in holding on their hats. The gentle can stands on a little platform, allows itself to be punched on the head, and after a few turns of a handle, is neatly scalped. I avoid most fresh foods because I cannot see to avoid worms. These unsavory creatures are absent from the citrus fruits and bananas, and from a few of the vegetables. But cooking vegetables on an electric plate takes a long time, and the food which I cook is not always well done.

My canned goods, when they arrive, are immediately "catalogued" and "filed" for future reference. I have worked out a system by which I can locate any given variety at any time, and with accuracy. I arrange all cans alphabetically on the shelves. Vegetables, for instance, begin with asparagus, followed by beans—baked, lima, string, wax—then beets, Brussel sprouts, and so on. Canned fruit starts with apricot, and goes along to raspberry, and fruit has a special shelf. Cans of fish and meat are different in shape, so that there is no confusion. I know exactly where each can is, and if there is a gap next to the asparagus, the further can will be lima beans, the open space indicating that the baked beans have been eaten.

When my supplies are delivered, the grocery boy obligingly names each can as he hands it to me, and in this way I am enabled to put it at once in its proper place on the shelf.

In this arrangement of cans, I learned the necessity of doing things for myself. One of my earliest experiences in living alone was when a friend put away a number of cans in the pantry for me. That night I decided to have pea soup for dinner, because the weather had turned damp and cold. There was only one can of soup, and its place on the shelf was at the extreme right, beyond the row of vegetables. I opened the can so placed, and discovered that it contained asparagus. I poured it into a bowl and put it in the icebox. I took the second can on the right end. The contents came out with a "blop." I tasted it, and found coconut. I was a bit dazed. But I had decided that pea soup was the menu, and pea soup it should be if every can remaining had to be opened and the icebox filled with bowls. After concentrated thought, I suddenly remembered that my friend was left-handed, and so had put asparagus on the right; ergo, pea soup should be at the left. It was.

Cooking canned goods may sound stupid but it has its high spots. When the dinner hour draws near, I may say enthusiastically, "Tonight I'll have peas." That is, the main course will be peas, and if I'm not full some canned fruit will be added. When I don't feel particularly keen about anything, I say "Table d'hôte," and that interprets itself into the first can my hand touches, which, of course, is a surprise.

There are adventures, too. One such enterprise befell me on a Sunday night in July. I was sitting in the living room idly thinking about supper and recalling what was in the icebox—a can of lobster, a head of lettuce, a jar of French dressing. Bosh! I was tired of salads; I had eaten one every day for a week. Lobster? It would be nice to go to Delmonico's and have a broiled live lobster and a glass of Pol Roger. I dreamed on for a few minutes, then gave myself a mental shake. "Wake up, you idiot," I said to myself, "Delmonico is gone and you are only half here."

This silent wail did not create an appetite for lobster salad; I sat a while longer and then came the idea. I rose from the chair with alacrity and determination, hurried to the icebox, grabbed the can and opened it. I put a generous lump of butter in a low pot and when it was sizzling put in the pieces of lobster, sprinkled a spoonful of curry powder on top, opened a bottle of beer, turned the radio on for the dinner music from the Waldorf, and chuckled over my supper. It was novel and good.

There are strict limitations on my cooking. Some of these I recognize before I start, others I have to acknowledge after several failures. I refuse to do a thing halfway. It must turn out successfully or go into the discard.

For example, I've never prepared scrambled eggs properly. I've beaten them and poured them into a hot buttered pot, the result being a mass of dry lumps, quite disagreeable. I've tried the French way in hot cream, and the results achieved are either a slippery underdone affair, or a separation of tiny lumps floating in a watery liquid. A dish of scrambled eggs has never resembled the smooth, light, dreamy affair which is served even in ordinary restaurants, nor the appetizing ones I had made when I could see. My scrambled eggs are not up to standard, so after numerous failures, I have decided that it can't be done.

An omelet, one of those fluffy brown on the outside and delicately cooked inside, also is beyond my capabilities. Successful egg dishes are strictly confined to coddled, timed by my Braille watch, or hard boiled. A bit zestless, but a variation from canned stuff.

During my culinary exploits, I often think of a story of a blind couple that was told to me by an old friend, shortly after my coming home from the hospital. The blind man had a small business of his own and his wife did all the housework including cooking, laundering, mending, and taking care of their two children, one a baby and the other two years old.

At that time, the story was most encouraging to me, for if a woman with very little education could do so much, I ought to be able to do a bit more, when my strength returned, although housework at that period was not necessary.

Housework did become necessary. I tackled cooking and light housework—and then tackled my old friend.

"Peter," I said sternly, "do you remember telling me a story about a blind couple you knew?"

"Yes."

"Suppose you give me an unexpurgated version now."

He chuckled, "All right. Let me say, by way of preface, that I have eaten in lumber camps and tenement houses. I say this to show you that I'm not overparticular. I couldn't eat in that house. I liked those blind people and it hurt me to refuse to sit down at their table, because my refusal hurt their feelings." He paused, then said reminiscently, "I tried it once. Do you want me to describe the soup?"

I shook my head. Women who have been blind since childhood have been trained in State schools to cook, sew, launder, and clean, and later do these things in their homes. Revised versions of their accomplishments are given to me as inside information and are respected as such.

The variation in standards of cleanliness is not confined to the blind—people who can see don't look on cleanliness eye to eye.

New acquaintances usually fail to understand my stressing the importance of allowing me to do things for myself. They insist on making tea and washing the cups and saucers afterward. At four o'clock—I always have tea at four—one of these women will jump up and say, "Sit still. I'll do everything. Just tell me where the tea is." The little scene is almost without variation. I say that the tea is in the left corner of the lowest shelf. The woman has rushed to the kitchen and in a minute calls, "It isn't here." Thereupon I go to the kitchen and put my hand on the tea canister.

"Oh, I was looking on the wrong shelf. How wonderful of you to know where things are."

I have yet to encounter any person who listens or remembers a simple direction for one minute. After a number of such experiences I decided that it was easier to say sternly that I preferred doing the things myself.

On one occasion I played the part of a Rube Goldberg cartoon heroine. I had given up my bedroom to a friend for her out-of-town visitor. It is pleasant to be of use to someone, my usual role being one of acceptance. The new guest proved to be interesting, and our slight contacts, for she was out most of the time, were a pleasure. I told her not to feel that she had to stay in her room, that the chairs in the living room were more comfortable than the ones in her room, and that the piano and the telephone were at her disposal. But never, never, must she go into the kitchen, and I followed this seemingly cantankerous order by a clear explanation.

Everything went smoothly until Sunday. I went out early Sunday morning and didn't return until seven. I went to the kitchen to make tea, and my hand touched a saucer on the table. It belonged under the cup on the third shelf, so I put up my left hand to feel the place and found it empty, not even the cup there. I always have to feel a spot before putting anything down so that nothing else gets knocked off in the process. In this particular case a misplaced cup and saucer didn't make much difference, there were others in the china closet.

But before getting them I went to the icebox to get butter and jam. On the way I stumbled over a tin cracker box on the floor. I picked it up. It was quite heavy and rattled when I shook it, and on examination it was found to contain bolts and screws. This box belonged on a high shelf, which required mounting a chair or steps to reach. I am no longer a chamois, neither is a chair a crag, but the idea is somewhat similar, so that I decided to put the tin box on the drainboard and let someone else put it away later. My outstretched left hand on the drainboard felt an oval Pyrex dish, whose proper place was on the second shelf below the cup-and-saucer corner. On this spot my guiding hand discovered the teapot and teaball, their place being on the shelf over the range.

It was then that a Goldberg cartoon came into my mind, and I chortled. If I hadn't kicked the tin box, hadn't tried to put it on the drainboard, hadn't found there the Pyrex dish, the teapot would not have been found at all.

Not only do I have to teach my friends to leave kitchen utensils alone, but I have to teach them to engineer me in strange surroundings. New pupils are timid and old ones forget that I am blind.

But to get back to routine!

The childhood habit of being freshly dressed after luncheon still persists, so that I always change from morning to afternoon dress. Once I thought, "What is the use of all this formality? Why not flop around in morning clothes? No one really cares about my appearance." It took some arguing with myself to silence my own suggestion, but I realized that if I let myself slip, even a little, I would grow lazy and sloppy.

In reference to dressing, it is the lesser objects that cause the most trouble. These are the things that I used to choose by sight. In some way, I have to know the color of stockings, gloves, scarves, and handkerchiefs.

The first step in simplification was to have fewer of each article. Handkerchiefs are safe because they are all white. A dozen pairs of stockings, divided into two shades of six pairs each, are enough at one time. I buy a half dozen pairs, when a preceding set of six has worn out. Six or eight pairs of gloves suffice. These must be washable, as I prefer light beige or white, although after my first ride in the subway, when I grasped banisters going down and up steps and my companion told me of the result, I decided to wear black when traveling where handrails had to be wiped. This is not a criticism of subway housekeeping, but a confession of my own laziness.

White gloves are kept in a box. The others go into a corner of the drawer. Unlike stockings, gloves do not get washed every morning, but they do get washed a pair at a time, to keep them matched.

Stockings are only mixed on my return from a visit. Then a number of pairs are washed in one swoop, and when they are dry some friend will separate the colors. Whereupon the daily, one-pair-at-a-time routine starts all over again.

The number of scarves is limited to four—a black-and-white, a white, a purple, and a gray. They are of different materials and thus each color can be identified. Once I surprised an old friend when I said I would wear a gray scarf and went to the chiffonier drawer and picked it out.

"How wonderful," she exclaimed. "It is gray. How did you know it? You've certainly got a sixth sense?"

"No," I said, "gray is the only woolly scarf I possess and there isn't any sixth sense in captivity."

That overworked "sixth sense" is frequently knocked into a mashed fedora by my simple common-sense explanation of the truth. Why think that I am wonderful? There is no compensation for lost sight. It is funny how people will insist in believing that we blind are miracle workers.

We must concentrate on actions that to other people seem infinitesimal. To remember that the gray scarf is wool, the black one velvet, is not a tax on my memory. It is a filing system in which each item bears an unseen ticket and nothing must ever be misplaced—furniture, cans, clothes.

I know how it appears to my friends, because I once lived in the world of sight, and therefore now understand their viewpoint as well as my own. They find what we do "wonderful," but I am both "they" and "we" and the only wonderful part is that "we" have to think and remember many details before we can act. "They" don't.

My method of living must be simple and direct. An unnecessary gesture means an extra difficulty. When I touch an object, I must recognize it, also its position in regard to the object wanted. People comment on the ease with which I find things, never realizing that this ease had been won by many, many hours of thinking and planning. Each thing in its proper place was an early lesson! I can't toss my coat over the back of a chair and instantly remember which chair it was when the coat is needed. I can't drop my handbag on couch, table, or chair and not spend fruitless minutes on a feeling tour. Every square inch of chair seats, length and breadth of tables and couch, must be touched and the search may extend to other rooms, including the kitchen, and I then find the bag on top of the refrigerator!

Chapter 7

Little by little the routine of my life indoors was established. It consisted chiefly in the round of daily tasks, the preparation of my simple meals, the bedmaking and the dusting, the ordering of my household supplies for the day. And for the lighter side, there were the visits of friends of all ages and stations, and the modest tea parties which I enjoyed giving, once I had mastered the art of handling a teapot and presiding at my own tea table, sans sight. But so far, practically my entire life was being lived indoors, and a day arrived when I began to desire the resumption of my normal activities in the world outside my apartment.

My grasping at a new idea for an adventure is only a gesture, because I don't dare act on impulse. An action may appear feasible, but even so it must be given careful consideration. First of all, fear must be trampled down—the fear of physical accidents, the fear of being unsuccessful, and the sneaking suggestion that the adventure might not be worth the effort. It would be so easy to stay safely at home. Whereupon I recalled the statistics that show that women meet with more accidents in their homes than abroad; and as I spent much more time in my apartment than outdoors, I decided that the percentage of safety lay with the outs.

I liked being hostess in my own home, but I also like being a guest. I appreciated having friends shop for things which could not be ordered by telephone. But also, I began to crave little shopping excursions on my own account. My home-cooked dishes were nourishing and adequate, but times came when I longed for a real meal in a pleasant restaurant. And so one fine day I made a resolve. To the very first person who should ask: "Will you come to dinner?" I would answer: "Thank you, I shall be delighted. Any particular night?" To the first person who would suggest a shopping trip, with me in personal attendance, I would respond with: "I'd love it. When do we start?"

My friend Trude was the first to suggest having dinner out with her. She confessed to me later that my prompt acceptance had somewhat floored her, and she had been about to add to her suggestion, "But I don't know how it can be managed." However, as I seemed to know what I was talking about, she supposed it was all right. She was afraid to come for me alone, when the time arrived, and she and her husband came together and took me the few blocks to their home in a taxi.

I never told of my own excitement at going somewhere without my husband or my son. The whole affair to me was one grand adventure. The unfamiliar apartment, where voices, even my own, sounded differently, a new chair, and a dinner that didn't come out of cans. Everything I touched at the table was different in weight or shape. The maid would stand beside me with a dish of vegetable, not knowing what to do until Trude would tell her to put some on my plate. But she was eager to do the right thing, and soon caught the idea of serving me.

This little venture broke the ice for all concerned. Trude quickly lost her nervousness with me, and from then on we frequently went out together. In fact, she so far forgot my blindness that one day she telephoned and asked me to go to a fashion show!

When my other friends observed that I was venturing beyond the confines of my home, there were many offers of escort to restaurants, to shops, to parties, and to places of entertainment.

I had several very amusing experiences during these first excursions into the outside world. One of the most amusing was with a man who was escorting me home from an evening party. The man knew the neighborhood, and had to walk only three blocks. He was interested in some subject and was talking rapidly. For no particular reason that I could understand, he suddenly stopped talking and walking. There was a brief pause, and then came the ejaculation: "Dammit, where are we?"

I laughed. "Well, where are we?"

"I don't know."

He sounded so concerned that I asked quietly: "What do the street signs say?"

I felt him turn and twist. Finally he said: "Christopher and Seventh Avenue."

We had gone south instead of north. I told him how to get me home, which was quite simple, but he began to talk and again we got lost. At this point I took a stand.

"Stop talking until we get home!" I commanded firmly, and so by dint of maintaining strict silence, we completed the remainder of the journey in safety.

A similar experience with another man taught me to listen to conversation with one ear and to keep the other cocked for traffic sounds. I know New York well, and I learned to make a mental note of what streets we crossed. A companion is usually surprised at my sureness, but I learned it in self-defense.

An incident in illustration of this occurred once when I was walking with a friend from the I.R.T. subway at 40th Street and Seventh Avenue to Lord and Taylor's. Traffic sounds told me that we were on the south side of the street, and when we neared Sixth Avenue my friend said: "The lights are against us on the Avenue, so we will cross the street."

"Why?" I asked, "Lord and Taylor's is on Thirty-ninth. We go south, not north."

My friend was puzzled for a moment, and then said: "You're right. I'd have gone in the wrong direction. How did you know where we were?"

"How did I know?" I responded. "I *have* to know!"

All this was very amusing, and my trips around my own neighborhood and uptown with my friends were pleasant and stimulating.

But there came a day when I sat down and did some heavy thinking. I realized that my dependence on my friends was utter and complete. I acknowledged that they were charming and behaved as though it were a pleasure to do things for me. But my common sense was at work and I faced facts. When a hostess invited me to her house, she had to arrange for my transportation or come for me herself. In the latter case she would not only spend twenty minutes coming for me and another twenty minutes taking me to her home, but there would be the return engagement. An hour and twenty minutes, plus the time wasted in changing her house clothes for street things. This was all wasted motion. Was there any way to avoid it? Obviously I could refuse invitations, but going out gave me so much pleasure that I was unwilling to forego it. So what? The same proposition held good in going shopping with me. I slowed the performance and wasted their time. Another "so what?" and it was up to me to find a solution.

My appreciation of the loving kindness shown me was a deep and heartfelt gratitude, but this did not alter the fact that I was in danger of falling into a way of imposing on friends. This I felt I must not allow to happen. I sat down to work the problem out, and finally hit upon the solution by accident.

It was a combination of circumstances, an appointment with a doctor, and a friend who had found difficulty in keeping her engagement with me. We were riding in a taxi which we had taken from a stand near my apartment, while she told of the arrangements she had been forced to make at home. I felt sunk—and then suddenly found the answer I had been seeking, and the way to freedom. A taxi for myself. I asked what our driver looked like and the reply being favorable, I asked him his name and if I could reach him by telephone. And so began a new life.

It is difficult for me to explain the full meaning of my discovery of a taxi and its owner, Joseph Lynch.

Blindness had continuously thwarted my physical activities, and still checks many of them. To break its bonds, to leave the safety of my home without being in the care of a solicitous friend, was a momentous decision. It meant not only freedom of the body, but also a free spirit. I had suffered from the consciousness that I, who had once been efficient, had become a burden. I acknowledged that no one had ever acted as though I were a burden, but that didn't prevent me from knowing that I was. Therefore, my spirit soared with the new idea, and the first time that I went out in the taxi alone was a great adventure—the greatest adventure of my blind years.

I prepared for the event with meticulous care; I wrote a shopping list on the typewriter, although the list was not long nor its items important; I powdered my face and used lipstick, put an extra polish on my nails, pinned back loose ends of hair, and adjusted my suit with pulls and pats. I really couldn't have been more particular if I had expected to meet a personage.

I had telephoned for Lynch and when he rang the bell I clicked the door button and Lynch waited for me at the foot of the stairs. I may or may not have pranced down the steps, but I felt like it.

Lynch drove me to McCreery's and turned me over to John, the doorman. I had known John by sight for thirty years and felt quite safe. John led me into the shop and stood me up against a counter. Someone rang for the section manager. He telephoned for a personal shopper, and I started off with a strange young woman who had never before encountered a blind person. We both had a good time because she was interested and I was amused. This performance has been repeated quite often and I always get a thrill out of it.

As a rule, saleswomen, like my friends, are unable to describe designs. In fact, in answer to my question, they become speechless. For a saleswoman to become speechless may seem unbelievable, but it is true in my case.

Table linen is safe so far as color is concerned because it is always white. But I fear the stiff ungraceful fleur-de-lis flourishes on my damask despite my efforts for more original patterns.

With draperies, I now confine my inquisitiveness to color of the background and the predominant color of the design. The form of the design is beyond anyone's description.

Nevertheless, color is sometimes of paramount importance, particularly in wearing apparel. A saleswoman assured me that a housecoat was a soft rose color. One of my friends on seeing it said it was red, another said it was scarlet, and yet a third said it was raspberry. What I am sure of is that it is comfortable and not black.

Of course, all these objects, including china and glass, are handed to me to feel. I run my finger around a plate which doesn't tell me a thing, feel the shape of a cup which doesn't tell me its color, and trust that the effect on my table is not too bizarre.

After such a shopping adventure, my personal guide takes me back to Lynch and I leave with a warm memory of the interest and helpfulness displayed by section managers and salespeople.

Lynch, to my delight, was alert and quick to learn, although a steering wheel and a blind person are not in the least alike. In fact, the management of one is the direct opposite of the method used for the other. Yet he drives well and guides well. When he calls for me, he waits at the foot of the stairs until I come down. He then holds the front door open and leads me through with his left hand. In the vestibule we shift sides so that I can take his right arm. He never fails to mention the steps, leads me across the sidewalk, and carefully puts me in the car. He knows my customary stopping places uptown, McCreery's, the Park Lane, and the dentist's office, and downtown he knows the address of the American Foundation for the Blind, 15 West 16th Street, and the whereabouts of several friends. He is permitted to wait for me, even though parking may not be allowed ordinarily. He brings me home, comes upstairs and unlocks my door. I feel quite safe with Lynch.

The taxi, Lynch, and I having proved to be a workable combination, I decided to buy a dress in a shop, because the establishment which had made my clothes for years had gone out of business. I consulted my friends. From the information gathered, I chose Bergdorf Goodman's, which was unknown to me. I had also learned that in the shop there was a Miss Ann Goodman who was "very understanding."

Armed with this slight clue, I used my ally, the telephone. I asked the operator for Information, asked Information for Bergdorf's number, and on getting it I asked for Miss Goodman.

The charming voice that answered me bolstered up my faith in a seemingly mad undertaking. I explained my condition and asked for the name of a saleswoman who would grasp the situation. After that I would be responsible for the choice of gown. Miss Goodman assured me that she would take care of me herself. It was just as simple as that.

I drove to the shop and, as the doorman didn't seem to know exactly what to do, the watchful Lynch climbed down off his seat and helped. Inside the shop we were met by a hostess, I presume, who took me to the second floor. As we stepped off the elevator, a voice said, "Good afternoon, Mrs. Bretz. Miss Goodman will be here in a moment. She left word that she was to be called as soon as you came."

I am delighted with my dress and so are my friends, but there was an added touch of thoughtfulness which I appreciated. I was wearing an old necklace of jet and gold, and when the new gown was tried on, Miss Goodman said, "That is a handsome necklace but it doesn't look well with this dress." To me that little remark is the prettiest part of the experience. It showed that

Miss Goodman knew that I wanted to look right and that I couldn't know that my necklace spoiled the effect. I cherish the kindly spirit of that suggestion, and its memory will long outlast the garment.

The success of shopping, instead of satisfying me, merely stimulated by adventurous spirit to push on. The next idea was to try lunching alone in an uptown hotel. I had enjoyed lunching at the Park Lane with friends on previous occasions. Therefore when, on a bright December day, the spirit of adventure seized me, abetted by my old liking for a quiet dining room, well-trained waiters, and soft-voiced guests, I telephoned Lynch and instructed him to call and drive me to the 48th Street entrance of the Park Lane. This entrance was nearer the dining room than the Park Avenue door.

Arriving at the correct hour for luncheon, Lynch led me from the taxi to the corridor leading to the dining-room steps. Georges, the maitre d'hôtel, saw me at once and came forward. He took my arm and conducted me to a table at the side of the room where I could sit on a bench. My first experience with Georges, four years earlier, had shown me that he was familiar with the difficulties of blindness.

Everything went smoothly. Georges, with customary suavity, suggested dishes easy for me to handle and, more than that, watched to see that they were properly presented to me. The first course was fruit suprême. The fruit was in a small bowl set in a silver epergne, which the waiter placed on my plate. The next instant Georges took it and removed the bowl, put it on the plate, and said quietly, "Madame can hold this with her fingers." Georges never asked but once if I would like a cocktail. He knows that I want a dripped Pernod and it is served without my ordering it.

Luncheon had proved to be so successful an adventure that I was tempted to try the more difficult one of dinner. Yielding to a temptation for fun which affects no one but myself is a jolly kind of entertainment. There is the conception, the planning, and the accomplishment. The idea forms as a joke and produces a chuckle; a successful result gives me inordinate pride, which is another joke. The only real obstacles are in the carrying out of my wish.

In the question of dinner the first difficulty was transportation. Unfortunately, Lynch is off duty at night, so that a Western Union messenger must come to my aid. My body is like a piece of furniture and arrangements must be made to cart it around. This is a bit annoying. To get to the Park Lane would be easy enough with Lynch, but to return home with an unknown taxi man and accompanied by a messenger boy seemed more complicated. And then there was the picture of a Western Union uniform walking up to my table and escorting me out of the dining room! It simply wasn't being done, so what? I mentioned the matter to Lynch, when we were on a shopping tour, and with his ready coopera-tion he said that he would stretch his day and wait for me.

This point having been settled, I chose a pleasant evening and prepared for the event. I dressed as carefully as though I were young and preparing to go out with my fiancé. My out-side appearance was that of a dignified gray-haired woman in a long-sleeved black dinner gown, but inside, where no one could see, I was a six-year-old with a box of chocolates.

As the dinner was not just eating, but dining, I decided in favor of food that is not on my everyday bill of fare. I began with raw osyters. The waiter removed the glass of tomato cocktail from the center of the plate and put a gob of horse-radish and a few drops of lemon juice on each oyster. A raw oyster, to me, is merely a ski to carry a horse-radish jumper. Judging by my throat, the fellow who won that particular race wore a bright-red sweater.

Georges cut my meat and hearts of lettuce, and at the end spread ripe, leaky Camembert on crackers, the kind of Camembert that couldn't be kept in an apartment. It would have to roost on the fire escape, whereat neighbors would protest.

Throughout the dinner hour, the violinist slid sentimentally along the strings and the saxophone gave an excellent imitation of the sob stuff of a cello. They played modern music, and languorous waltzes in an old-fashioned manner— or is it still in style? I felt about twenty-two years old and had a beautiful time.

Lynch brought me home safely and after I had put away my coat and hat, pocketbook and stick, I sat down in the chair by the flowers and thought over the pleasant evening and wished that it could be repeated once a month. It was not just the food and change of atmosphere, it was the adventure, too. A dinner out of cans? Pooh!

Every escapade carried through successfully adds to my courage and my sense of freedom. The latest one also opened up an avenue to new adventures which I may try at will.

The idea came on a morning when there was nothing in the icebox that I really wanted for lunch. I thought of the Park Lane, but I wanted more than food. I wanted music, too, and at that time the Park Lane didn't have music at the luncheon hour. Well, what about the Waldorf? I had been there with friends but never alone. I actually gasped. The idea seemed brilliant and daring. I just had to try it. I picked up the telephone and called the Waldorf, asked for the dining room and reserved a table. I was tremendously excited and the responsive Lynch shared my excitement. We dashed uptown and he carefully turned me over to the doorman, who led me into the hotel. There, as though by magic, a strange man grasped my arm and guided me up some steps. At the top a hostess took charge and conducted me to a table. The orchestra was playing and I couldn't help walking to its rhythm.

The waiter didn't know about reading a menu aloud and I didn't ask him to. I ordered deviled crab and artichoke vinaigrette, a favorite combination of mine which it is impossible for me to have in my apartment. I lingered over coffee and on the way home kept saying to myself, "I did it—I did it—I did it!"

Later that afternoon I sat by the window and grinned over my absurd elation. For it is absurd when a grown person can't drop into a restaurant and have luncheon without getting excited about it. But to me in my blindness, the vital significance of doing a thing is more important than the thing itself. That's why life is amusing.

Much as I enjoyed my excursions to the Park Lane and to the Waldorf, I realized that my pocketbook wouldn't stand the strain of frequent visits there. I also realized that thinking of them would not add flavor to my home food. Dinner out of cans is bound to become distasteful at times, and I was forced to think of a more economical alternative for eating at home. I found it in the Waverly Inn. Accordingly, when my own food preparations pall, and my palate whimpers for a slice of roast meat, fresh vegetables, and a dessert that isn't canned fruit, I telephone to this near-by restaurant. My call is answered by a pleasant voice saying: "Waverly Inn."

"This is Mrs. Bretz," I announce.

"Oh, hello, Mrs. Bretz," comes back the voice. "Are you hungry?"

"Starving to death," I assure her.

"I'll send Howard right over."

It is just as simple as that, and in a few minutes Howard, the bus boy, comes for me, acting as though this extra task were a pleasant one.

His manner creates an excellent mood for the enjoyment of an excellent dinner. He has learned to remind me of gutters, steps, and doormats.

My special waitress, whom I have dubbed "La Blonde," reads the menu to me, and if it contains one of my favorite dishes—veal, lamb, or fried eggplant—there is a happy note in her voice. She is thoughtful, too. She breaks crisp rolls into small pieces and butters them, and lightly mentions that she is putting a dish before me. I am not personally acquainted with Albert, the chef, but he sends my meat cut up and never puts tomato sauce on my food because I don't like tomato. Such invariable kindness, for it is invariable, is astonishing. Other people pay the same price for dinner that I do but my blindness seems to bring out a special consideration which they do not receive. There is an atmosphere of leisureliness about the Inn and its garden, no rushing and clattering, no loud talk. I like dining there.

There are many convenient shops in Greenwich Village, near where I live, and among them there is a famous silversmith. I first became acquainted with him and with his work when I ran up against a problem which he eventually solved for me. The problem concerned a Braille watch that I had obtained through the American

Foundation for the Blind. My watch was without trimmings. It had a hunting case, as there is no crystal to protect its hands. The hours are marked by dots, and the minute hand is long, so that it is easy to distinguish from the shorter hour hand. I put it in my handbag, dropped the bag, and the watch went to a repair shop. I had a pocket made in a belt, and took off my skirt without remembering the watch. There followed a "click" on the floor.

I said, "Tut," and again, "Tut," but the remark didn't make the watch go, except back to the repair man. It was evident that an addition would have to be made either to my mind or to the timepiece, and the latter seemed more feasible.

I carefully considered the problem. Most things are problems with me and if they're not problems, they are situations. At any rate they require a lot of thought, assisted by a cigarette. The watch problem was solved, or rather the first part of it, by my recalling a fob I had worn in my girlhood, but where in these days could a watch fob be found? I inquired among my friends, only to draw a blank. At last a woman suggested having one made and mentioned Jo Michels, a silversmith in this neighborhood.

I immediately sought him out and was delighted when he let me handle his lovely trinkets and was still more delighted with his creation of a fob. It is a disk with a bee mounted on it. A bee stands for my initials—A.B. A neat idea. I also possess other pieces made by Michels. It is gratifying to have some of his beautiful workmanship and original designs.

Through friends in the Village I became acquainted with the French pastry shops in their vicinities, and am now a connoisseur of napoleons and brioche and know where the best are to be bought. These patisseries, the Hawthorn Flower Shop, a wine shop, and Paul's, the green grocer's, are now on my Braille telephone list. I'm apt to forget the seasons for certain vegetables and flowers and ask for the impossible, but I don't get it. The wine shop isn't temperamental, and a man there obligingly draws the long corks from bottles because I don't make a clean job of it.

I am convinced that the secret of the success of my adventures lies in the honesty of my approach to those with whom I come in contact on these excursions. I say, "I am blind. Will you help me?" and difficulties disappear as though by magic. Wherever I go, everyone shows me consideration. There is a let-me-help you sound in voices that makes my world glow with friendly warmth.

I would be unable to cope with the unexpected without the help of these kind people. I know that, and put my trust in doormen, waiters, salespeople, and, inspired, they never let me down.

The fear of being unsuccessful is only a matter of pride, for I also learn something through failure. Two outstanding failures were the experiments of going to the Flower Show and an art exhibition. I went to the first with a city friend who didn't know gardens, or names of most ordinary flowers. I might as well have been looking at elephants. At the second, the artist himself came to my aid. But, alas, when he described a landscape I asked what kind of trees. It was a tactless question, because he didn't know!

Chapter 8

I haven't left New York, except for short visits, since I have been blind, so it is a fair assumption that I am still here. Nevertheless, the city in which I now live is not the one I knew when I could see. The change has not been gradual; it has been violent and complete.

I have lived in New York or near by for thirty-five years, and visited here as a girl. I knew Delmonico's of the shaded lamps and delicious cuisine. Sherry's dining-room furniture was so distasteful to me that I never appreciated the cooking. What is wrong with the atmosphere of some dining rooms?

In those days Fifth Avenue was delightful on a winter afternoon. There would be a scattering of well-dressed people, women wearing furs, men wearing high hats, going somewhere for tea. Little knots of friends would gather, talking in low, well-bred voices. There was no hurry, no rush of last-minute shoppers, no crowds. A short walk along the Avenue created an appetite for tea and toasted muffins. A man seldom, very seldom, ordered a cocktail. If he were that type, he was not supposed to be in a tearoom, but at a bar. I have watched drinking habits change, too, and am called old-fashioned because I never take more than one cocktail before a meal. I still consider a cocktail an *apéritif*, and suspect that those who use them otherwise don't appreciate their significance.

I knew Lord and Taylor's and Arnold Constable's when they were on Broadway, and 23rd was the shopping street. Tiffany and Schirmer were on Union Square, and Thorley on 28th Street west of Broadway.

In this neighborhood the theatrical district began with Weber and Field's on Broadway. Once I was taken there to a revival. A Weber-and-Field revival must not be confused with the camp-meeting variety. The Weber-and-Field audience was composed of men with a slight scattering of women, a mixture quite unlike other theaters, and made me feel a little out of place.

When Lillian Russell appeared on the stage I thought she was as beautiful as the Venus de Milo, the goddess being at that time my ideal of perfection. That she flatted her notes and sometimes sang off key didn't detract from her beauty. No one on the stage could sing or dance and no one cared. Everyone's appearance was greeted with loud applause; the hand clapping of men makes a terrific noise. It was like a house party where some of the guests did stunts to please themselves and amuse their friends. One attendance was enough.

This downtown theatrical district moved farther up Broadway. Fifth Avenue shifted from residences to shops. The uptown trek was gradual and despite all the changes there was no sudden wrench in our lives. New York was still New York, the city I preferred above all others in America.

Nor have I lost interest in New York since I can no longer see it, and it is not the city I once knew. That New York was as completely demolished for me as though suddenly obliterated by a hurricane, and in its place there is a city without color, without perspective, without form. There are no buildings, which means no beauty or variation of architecture, no lighted windows, no traffic lights to penetrate the murky atmosphere in which I move. The city, for me, lies under a London pea-soup fog, a fog through which no object can be seen; no shadow falls across my path. There is only an impenetrable something that is not the black darkness of an unlighted room or of a stormy night.

I Begin Again

I remember that black darkness, and though blind people customarily speak of living in the dark, my experience is like straining to look for an object through mud. The object can't be found, and the only thing to be seen is mud—the dirty tan of a pea-soup fog. This atmosphere is filled with the danger of unseen obstructions or human bodies. Collisions occur, even though I am always accompanied by a friend. I never go out alone except in a taxi, and then the driver is responsible for my safety.

Strange voices accost me on the street. Sometimes the owner of a voice knows me, although I fail in my recognition. Gradually, voices are beginning to have individuality.

An unrecognized voice caused me a surprise about five years ago. A friend was bringing me home one Sunday afternoon and as we neared the corner of Bank Street she exclaimed, "Hello, there, where did you come from?"

A man's voice answered, "Hello, yourself, I'm in this neighborhood once in a while."

"But not on Sunday afternoon, surely?"

There were a few more words, and I listened, waiting for the man to be introduced. Then the masculine voice said, "Hello, Mother."

Needless to say, I've known my son for quite a number of years, and with sight would have recognized him instantly, even on the Sahara. But this unexpected meeting, when I thought he was on Long Island, made me realize how much I had depended upon my eyes.

A newly blinded adult must not be confused with a person born blind. We have to learn to substitute our other senses for our sight and it is a slow process.

It is this substitution that makes New York queer to me. I have to be told what street I am on, although there is an atmospheric difference between Third Avenue and Park. Apartment houses where friends live no longer differ in facades, but only in entrances and hallways to elevators. Some entrances are level, some have a step up or down, and halls vary in a similar manner, unless they are tricky enough to have steps in groups. Elevators are all alike and the operators are all thoughtful in bringing the cage on a level with the floor.

To me an apartment now consists of drawing room and dining room. Undoubtedly there must be other rooms but I am able to make a sharp distinction between what I knew in the past and what I know now. It is this ability to recognize this difference that helps make blindness an adventure. Now I know when I am in a drawing room by the type of chair I sit in, but can have

no idea about the rest of the furniture, unless my
hostess mentions it. I have learned to become
acquainted with certain chairs, because a hostess
usually puts me in the chair occupied by me on
my first visit. She wants me to feel at home, a
warm and kindly thought.

Besides apartment houses, New York contains
only a few shops and several restaurants. I recognize each by its doorman's genial voice. Some of
these I greet by name, as they inquire after my
health.

This New York is wonderfully friendly. The
sympathetic voice is without a face. It speaks
from a specific height in the air in front of me.
Occasionally it is accompanied by a helping hand.
A friendly stranger will cross the street with me
and my companion to see us safely to the opposite sidewalk. A friendly stranger will hold a
door open for us, and friendly strangers will wait
at the top or bottom of steps to see that we don't
fall. The pea-soup fog is seasoned with human
kindness.

But the strangest aspect of all streets is their
emptiness. I pass only a scattering of people,
either uptown or in this neighborhood. There is
never a crowd. The emptiness was particularly
noticeable on Fifth Avenue a short time ago when
a friend and I walked down from Lord and Tay-

lor's to 12th Street. Trude is tall and easy to walk with. She is observant, sure, and, best of all, remembers to tell me about gutters. We walked at a swinging pace, interrupted only at cross streets when traffic was against us. As we crossed 13th Street, Trude said, "I'm thankful to get you safely through those crowds. I've never seen the Avenue so jammed."

Her remark and tone of relief surprised me, although my memory of Fifth Avenue at one o'clock on a bright day should have told me of the condition, but memory has been trained not to speak unless asked to. When Trude and I had paused on a corner, I had been conscious of two or three people near us, but I had been unaware of any crowd.

Chief of the causes contributing to my lack of consciousness of crowds are the necessity of concentrating on the occupation of the moment and the ability not to listen to sounds. Comparing crowds of the past with those of the present, I understand the difference between crowds seen and unseen. It is this ability of comparison that permits a blinded adult to recognize the vast abyss between the normal world and the world of the blind.

My world today is a curiously unreal world, a place where I must wander alone and helpless, yet laugh.

Chapter 9

Friends have always meant much to me through life, but until blindness overtook me, I didn't consider them as my most cherished entertainment. Each friend shows me a new landscape, and we walk there together, talking of what we find and making discoveries. Friends have no age limit. The oldest is eighty, the youngest twenty, and the others float along in between. The younger ones are full of hopes and plans. Some of them marry, whereat I loudly applaud, for in my opinion marriage is the happiest life in the world, and my cheering is from the heart.

Most of the elders have left hope behind. Some of them possess acceptance, and others possess a religion that seems to put what hope they have in a life beyond. To the elders, the world today is all wrong. The young ones make the best of it by a shift of standards.

Older people telephone before they come, because they want to see me alone, but the youngsters have a way of bobbing in. I endeavor to keep

ages and interests separated. If there are too
many extremes during the day, my brain feels
somewhat like an accordion, and gives a gasping
"woof" as the last visitor departs.

I remember one afternoon when the collection
around the tea table consisted of an Anglo-
Catholic priest, a Methodist minister, a Jew,
and two women, one a theosophist and the
other, I don't know what. Each guest seemed to
have his or her mouth open, ready to hold forth
on his or her particular interest. Before anyone
could bolt, I grasped the conversational reins
firmly and drove them all along the road labeled
"Difficulties confronting educated Negroes."

The priest was large and heavy in build and a
bit slow in grasping a new thought. He had been
born and brought up in a small town, but had been
in New York churches for a number of years.

In response to my observation that an educated
Negro must find insurmountable obstacles to success or happiness, the priest began, and to my fancy
had his finger tips pressed together, "If Negroes
fully comprehended the meaning of sacramental
devotion—" The chair supporting the square
frame of the minister had given an omnious creak.

"For all types to be herded in Harlem," my
tone was bland, "the question of schools presents
a problem."

"The Harlem Hospital is a good institution," the Jew contributed. "I personally know of an interesting operation, a touch-and-go case. The patient—"

"Oh, don't talk about operations, Mr. Reubans," the second woman exclaimed. "They give me the horrors. I have enough trouble with colored maids. You can't depend on them, and if you don't watch them every minute the cleaning isn't properly done. Only last week she dusted the clock and now it won't run. I haven't the groggiest notion what she did to it, but I'll have to have it repaired. Colored people are such a nuisance."

The theosophist coughed protestingly and snatched at the second's pause. "Your maid may be a noble soul reincarnated as a servant."

This sounded like an approaching storm, and I produced an umbrella, figuratively speaking, in the shape of a suggestion that someone must need some hot tea.

The minister carried his cup to the tea wagon to have it refilled, and while on his feet made a statement in a voice pitched to fill a church.

"There would be no Negro problem, if people acted like Christians."

He picked up the cup and took a cooky, which he bit with a forceful crunch.

"Ahem," the priest cleared his throat. "Kindly be specific in your use of the word 'Christian.'"

There was a slight accent on the word "your."

The minister hastily swallowed the piece of cooky, and a crumb lodged on the way down. The result was a strangled cough which resembled a backfire.

"Drink some tea," I urged and continued speaking as the bark subsided to a splutter. "I meant Negroes who are professional men and artists, like Tanner. Tanner lived in Paris, and the French government bought several of his pictures for the Luxembourg Galerie. He had a standing with the art colony in Paris and Étretat, which would have been impossible in New York."

The theosophist asked a question about Tanner, and we two monopolized the conversation for the remainder of the tea hour.

After my friends departed the accordion gasped wo-oo-of.

Groups are not all difficult; indeed, they can be jolly with laughter, funny stories, and music.

One evening two young married couples and a younger engaged couple gathered in the living room. The fiancée has a trained lyric soprano. Someone asked her to sing and without moving from her chair, she sang, "Only a Rose," from

The Vagabond King. Her lovely voice floated through the room, while my son accompanied her on the piano. He faked the accompaniment of her next choice, "Willie the Weeper." This ballad incited the other guest to do "My Name is Samuel Hall," and more of the same class. It would be stretching numerous points to suggest that they sang, because none of the others had musical voices, but they enjoyed themselves and amused me. There were also more light-opera songs. A few hours of sheer nonsense are a relief after discussions on economics, capital and labor, politics or war. Such objects pass the time, but I do like to laugh.

The charm of individual friends gives me much happiness. One such friend has an apartment overlooking St. John's Gardens, and in warm weather we have supper on the brick terrace. The splashing fountains, the rustling leaves, and cooing pigeons create an atmosphere that is far removed from New York. The food is placed on a wicker table: iced melon, cold meat and salad with French dressing made with wine vinegar, a bottle of claret or chianti, French pastry, and Spanish coffee. The flower boxes are full of fragrant bloom. Marco Polo, the kitten, is tethered to a chair. This tethering is necessary; otherwise, when my hostess goes to the kitchen he will leap on the table. Polo seems to know that I can't see him.

After supper my friend will read to me. There is a lovely singing timbre in her voice and she chooses delightful books. When the sun no longer warms my face, and the quality of the air changes to the cool of dusk, and somewhere a sleepy bird querulously peeps, "Move over on your own branch," I know night has come. Then my friend says, "It's too dark to read out here. Shall we go inside?" We step through the French windows into the living room. Marco Polo, untethered, dashes up on the little sofa where I sit and we have a romp, and my friend will continue to read or we will talk of books until midnight.

The reading includes the week's book reviews, and if a book sounds interesting, she gets it. She has read to me Huxley's "Eyeless in Gaza," J. Middleton Murray's autobiography, and many others. Best of all are the modern Irish authors. I have a predilection for the Irish novels, created by my fortunate introduction to them through Corkery's "The Threshold of Quiet." It is a fragile, exquisite story, told with charming delicacy. It is in my mind like the memory of a fragrance. Every country has its recognizable style in literature, and Ireland is not an exception.

If a last chapter of a book were read to me, it seems to me that I would know if it were Irish. There is a wistfulness about the ending, something intangible like a breath of sadness or longing.

My friend Trude lives on 9th Street. It's exhilarating to visit her; she's a bit ahead of the minute. Her maid makes a good Martini, and I know a good one when I get it outside my own house, where I think it is the best. We have dinner and return to the living room for coffee and cigarettes. Trude tells me of her doings, which means a serial story to me, and I'm eager for the next installment. Midnight comes before we become conscious of time, and Trude brings me home.

Friends often try to describe other people to me, but the average person's description of other people is woefully misleading. It is so inadequate and incorrect that the images created in my mind probably bear no resemblance to the original. This lack of descriptive ability on the part of the ordinary individual I have discovered for myself, although the police must constantly experience such vagueness.

Personally, I really don't care what color hair and eyes a man has, or whether he is dressed in gray or brown. It is only personality that matters, and that is expressed in the voice.

When I could see, my impression of a woman was based on her surface appearance—a stylish costume, a pleasing face, nice manners, and a low pitched voice. Now that appearance has no value, I get a curious insight into the natural person, which thus far has proved correct. This is more than can be said of my former appraisals.

The physical aspect of a large hand grasping mine and a voice from a spot six feet in the air does not necessarily mean a big personality and I sometimes find myself responding to a small one.

One of my friends is very short, yet possesses so much innate dignity that I picture her as of magnificent proportions. Another woman, six feet tall and heavy, has such a petty nature that I never can remember her physical size, and once offered to reach for a piece of china from an upper shelf because, in my conception of her, she was incapable of reaching so high. A woman, said to be pretty, has shown me unvarying kindness; yet I do not trust her because of the meanness in her voice.

My impression of a personality is not the result of conscious study, or of weighing the qualities in a voice. It would be eavesdropping because a voice is unguarded, and betrays secrets. People frequently ask me what I think they look like, or how old I think they are. These are curious questions, and to me unimportant. The color of hair or the shape of a nose is not an indication of character. There is something else, something intangible that is difficult to put into words. Perhaps the nearest approach to an explanation came from a woman with whom I was talking of a mutual friend. She said, "You see a person as they think they are, or hope to be. It's a higher conception than we get from their actions."

This may be part of it, but there is another side that sounds uncanny. I sometimes get a flashback into a person's past. One such instance was with a young woman who has come into my life in recent years. I know nothing about her family or her education. She is herself, without background. Yet once when she was telling me of some childish escapade, I heard myself say, "You should not have done that. You were too delicate." We were both surprised at my words. Naturally, she asked how I knew she had been delicate, which happened to be true. I could give no reason for my remark, and have learned to accept these queer little visions. I try to keep them to myself.

In personal contact not being able to see a speaker is sometimes confusing. I cannot always tell whether a ponderous remark is a labored joke, or meant seriously, because the expression of the face conveys nothing to a blind listener. A half smile becomes a safe reply for me. But if positions are reversed and I tell the funny story, a smile of the listener is no answer at all. It is utterly useless for a person to receive my jokes with an appreciative smile. My listeners should give at least one "Ha!" Either people forget this little sound, or else my stories are not funny.

The handicap of blindness prevents lip reading, which is unconsciously practiced by people who can see. I find, therefore, that I catch the gist of a remark more slowly, just hearing what is said, than I did when my ears were aided by my eyes. If we can watch a speaker, we know the word before its sound reaches us. Blindness is also the cause of an apparent rudeness when I break in on a person's speech as he pauses a moment. I hear the pause. I don't see the next word forming, and ask people to pardon this seeming ill manner. My explanation startles them, because they forget that I am blind.

People depend on facial movements to express the meanings of their words. The timbre of a voice is indicative of personality, but rarely of emotion. A voice shoots at me through the pea-soup fog. If its owner is well known to me, I can guess the hidden meaning beneath the words. With a newcomer, this is impossible. Eyes may be twinkling with mischief, or full of tears. Facial muscles may express sterness, sympathy, weakness, strength, and many other emotions. None of these shows in the voice.

Then there is the facial mask. A man may have broken himself of the habit of scowling and in the effort kept his face immobile, and a woman may use make-up that hides her real character. Both may have acquired large vocabularies, but they have forgotten their voices which still hold the scowl and the cattiness. True, there are a few persons who have cultivated a speaking voice, but the marks of the cultivator's teeth are, as it were, visible to us who are blind.

One of the pleasantest things my friends do for me is to read aloud to me. Ted thinks that I ought to keep up with modern American authors, and he chooses those of their works he considers suitable as well as characteristic. Thus, I feel familiar with Hemingway's, "The Sun Also Rises," several of Scott Fitzgerald's, Falkner's, and a few of Thomas Wolfe's short stories—no, "short" isn't the word, but at least they weren't novels—and some beautifully written scenes from "Of Time and the River."

Ted's ability to skip is a miracle. He marks a book before bringing it to the house, and from his reading I get a good idea of an author's style.

Nevertheless, his skipping gets me into trouble when I mention some particular book. "Serenade," by Cain, is a good example.

Once or twice during the reading, Ted said that he would omit an unimportant bit so as to finish the book in an evening. Otherwise, the reading seemed uninterrupted. When I mentioned my enjoyment of "Serenade" to a friend, she was horified. "Is that in Braille? How ghastly! How did you happen to get hold of it?" I mentioned Ted. "The boy ought to have better sense. Why didn't you stop him?" I protested that there was nothing wrong with the book. It had been quite exciting. That was all.

Whereupon my friend said that she had glanced at the book in the library, and that nothing would induce her to read such filth. She mentioned a scene of which I was ignorant; tried another, of which I knew nothing. Yet Mr. Cain need not fear that Ted spoiled his "Serenade." On the contrary, it was a vivid, swift-moving, and strongly written story, and quite complete.

Ted reads widely, so from him I get variety. He brings the *New Republic* and *The New Yorker*, and reads articles that are interesting or amusing. He has over a hundred books on Byron, and when he read to me a life of Byron, he amplified points with excerpts from other books on the same subject. While he read me four or five volumes of the exquisite Japanese story, "Genji," I lived in eleventh Century Japan.

Friends enjoy reading what they like, and their choice is so varied that it broadens my mental outlook. They read serious articles on politics and religion, gay and dull novels, and humorous books. I refuse to listen to sad ones. True, they gallantly offer to read anything I want. But after a few trials, I learned to be chary about suggestions. One experience is never to be forgotten.

A friend brought in Corkery's "The Threshold of Quiet" and read the first chapter to see if I would like it. I was so delighted that she left the book with me. I thought over the people who read to me and to whom this book might appeal, and decided on a man who preferred quiet charm. On his next visit, he opened the book at my request and began to read. Before he turned a page, I knew he was bored. Nevertheless, he finished a chapter pleasantly, then closed the book and laid it aside, saying, "You are not interested, are you?" A rhetorical question, it

required no answer. And what could I have said?
A hostess's duty is not to bore a guest.

A week later, a young man came at eleven in
the morning. It is necessary to specify morning,
because my young friends often bounce in at
eleven at night. But this time it was morning,
and I offered the young man luncheon later if he
would read five short chapters. He delivered his
part, but it seemed to me that he felt cheated in
the payment.

Later on, a literary woman asked if there were
anything I would like to have read, whereupon
I expatiated on this love of a book. She suggested
that we take the volume, dine at a restaurant,
and go to her quiet apartment where she could
read to me without the interruptions that were
apt to occur in my home.

This program was carried out—through one
chapter. Then she closed the book and said,
"You are not interested in this, are you?" The
question had a familiar sound and required no
answer. What could I have said? A guest must
not impose on a hostess's kindness.

"The Threshold of Quiet" was brought back
and put in the bookcase, where it sat with all
its enchantment closed to me. Blindness is sometimes aggravating.

At last a young Irishman came to see me. Tom usually reads modern poetry, T. S. Eliot being his favorite author. But on this evening there was no book in his pocket, and he asked if I had anything. I told him about "The Threshold of Quiet," and he began to read, and was immediately caught by its charm, as I had been. There was a lilt in his voice as he read to the end of the story. That was a happy evening.

There is an epilogue to this tale. A month later, the literary woman telephoned and asked if she could borrow Corkery's "The Threshold of Quiet," as she wanted to read it because Padraic Colum had praised the author. On the telephone, I am neither hostess nor guest, and took meanish delight in saying that the book had been lent to me and had been returned.

Why couldn't a professional writer have appreciated the unusual without having to be influenced by the opinion of a fellow craftsman? Perhaps intellectual freedom isn't precious to everyone!

I have always enjoyed having friends read to me, even before I became blind. Nowadays, when someone closes a book and ends a visit, and leaves me alone with my thoughts, I go back in memory to some of those readings. In the old New York that I first remember, one of my most vivid recollections is of a little group of friends who used to get together from time to time to read the works of favorite authors.

"Leaves of Grass" occupied a prominent position on the desk in the studio, and when two or more congenial spirits gathered together in our apartment, someone was sure to read a favorite poem. The reader pulled out the tremolo stop, and his quivering voice slowly pronounced each word. Emphasis, or the underscoring of a line, was obtained by a wide-flung gesture of one arm. The gesture began by drawing the back of the hand across brimming eyes, the hand then described an arc until the arm was outstretched at right angles to the body. It was held in that position for a moment, then the elbow flexed, the shoulder grew limp, and the arm fell helplessly to the side of the chair. Another pause, and the hand was lifted up and rested on the arm of the chair.

I remember one night in particular. Victor Herbert happened to be there, although he didn't belong in this group. Mr. Herbert always treated me as though I were seven years old. He laughed at the things I said. His laugh was noisy, but jolly and kind. I liked him. His presence that night didn't prevent a reading. The poem chosen was the "Dandelion." The gesture came at the last line. A respectful silence was kept by the devotees until the hand was in place, but Mr. Herbert took a big gulp of beer. He turned to me and asked, "How do you like that, my dear?"

I knew that he was not referring to the drink, so I said, "It isn't true. A dandelion isn't simple, and it hasn't a trusting face. It's an impudent street urchin, a gamin. It's a pest, and everyone hates it and has it dug up and thrown away."

One of the devotees spoke in the tolerant tone of voice so irritating to youth. "When you are older, you will learn to appreciate Walt."

The first part of this prophecy came true— the passing years saw to that.

Among our many musical friends in those early days was Ethelbert Nevin. At the time of my son's birth, we were living in Paris, as were Mr. and Mrs. Nevin. I saw them frequently that winter, and they were very much interested in the coming baby. In fact, they officiated as godparents at the baptism in the American Pro-Cathedral on the Avenue de l'Alma.

The day of the christening, my husband and I celebrated by going to the Folies Bergères. Yvette Guilbert was on the stage that night and gave a perfect example of the effectiveness of restraint. She sat in a high-backed chair, scarcely moving. Occasionally her supple body swayed as though of its own volition, her hands would flutter a little, her lips formed words. Her brilliant eyes expressed all her emotions: a lifted eyebrow, a sidelong glance, a stare of surprise, then downcast lids, as though leaving a decision to the audience. She talked her songs. One of them was about confetti, and Mademoiselle described the unexpected places where it had lodged in her clothing. The mention of each particular spot dotted the auditorium with laughs. The audience didn't roar with laughter and drown her words; it was as though Yvette Guilbert were tossing pebbles into a pool and each falling stone resulted in a jet of appreciation.

The program included the pantomime, 'Chand d'Habit. I saw this play five months later in London. Beerbohm Tree put it on with a complete lack of French flair. Tree himself was too sophisticated to play the part of the vagrant, and the three notes of the musical street cry, 'Chand d'Habit, produced by the orchestra were meaningless and wrongly accented for the call of the Old Clothes Man.

Mr. Tree thought me too shy to tell him how much I had enjoyed the pantomime. I thought it polite to keep still.

While my friends furnish the source of my greatest entertainment, there are many other forms that add much pleasure to my life. I make a distinction between activities in which I participate and entertainments in which I sit still and listen. Among the sit-still variety, the opera comes first. I have always preferred it above any other form of entertainment. The combination of voice and orchestra is so completely satisfying, and an opera pleases me more than a symphony concert. Blindness has given opera a new balance for me. The orchestra has become more important, and voices are like instruments added to it. Their quality, unlike that of strings or wood winds, weaves through the music with an unearthly, liquid purity that holds me spellbound. I no longer see the singers; their physiques, their costumes, and their awkward movements do not distract me.

In listening to a familiar opera, memory puts the old stage setting before my eyes. I should like to hear *Faust* again, and recall the last performance I attended at the Paris Opera House, when my son was eight years old and accompanied me to hear his first opera. He had leaned out of the box, completely absorbed, until roused to life by the "Soldier's Chorus." At this he turned back to me and said in a puzzled tone, "That isn't new, Mother."

He imagined that this was the first performance of a new opera and was astonished at recognizing a familiar theme. I had played the "Soldier's Chorus" for him many times when he had wanted to march around the room with a flag, and he had frequently heard talk of plagiarism in music, as this was a topic often discussed at home.

He has never forgotten the experience of his first opera, and it seems to me that *Faust*, with its many melodies and action, is easy for a child to understand.

Next to operas, I like musical comedies. The friend who goes with me reads the program and describes the stage. Now that my son is grown up, I find him the most satisfactory companion for a theatrical performance. He reads a program in a low voice, and describes each scene in a few words.

Descriptive power varies tremendously with different people, and exercising it is a novel experience for most. They stutter and stammer, and usually mention unimportant details first. However, I manage to gain some idea, and depend on my imagination for the rest.

I noticed at the performance of *I'd Rather Be Right* that my impression was more vivid than that of people who could see George M. Cohan.

To me, he was President Roosevelt. He did not attempt to imitate the President's voice, but there was a hint of Rooseveltian rhythm and cadence in the sentences—and I could not see him. I am not acquainted with the President or with his Cabinet. So why shouldn't I believe a voice that said he was Chief Justice Hughes, as well as a voice that says, "This is Ted." My credulity made the illusion perfect, and added to the fun.

Voices no longer have faces. A voice in my living room may enter through the door or through the loud-speaker. The only differences are that the ones that come through the door shake hands and stay longer. Otherwise, their physical appearances rest in my imagination.

There are only a few minor differences between Edwin C. Hill, whose voice comes through the radio, and a man caller who speaks in my room. When the visitor shakes hands, from the size of his hand and the position of his voice in the air I can approximate his height. However, I know nothing about the color of his suit or tie, his hair and eyes, and the radio is no more informative on these subjects in regard to Mr. Hill.

Another entertainment, though infrequent, is the movies. There are three movie houses in the vicinity of my home, but I rarely venture out for this kind of sit-still entertainment unless to hear Nelson Eddy. I learned to enjoy his voice and interpretations, which are all of him I know, on the radio. His manner is pleasant, and he sings as though he liked to sing. I feel as though he were one of my son's friends who stops in for little visits.

It was from Eddy performances that the realness of one radio personality was brought home to me. The program is long, and there are a number of artists on it. Perhaps they amuse some people, but they do not entertain me, so that I turn the radio off until time for Eddy's next song. It is not possible for me to gauge time accurately, so that often I turn the gadget too soon. Thus, on several occasions I heard an impudent boy, one Charles McCarthy, whose indulgence in personal remarks was encouraged by the applause of the studio audience. I used to turn the radio down until Charlie's chatter was only a buzz. It never occurred to me that he was a puppet, and when I learned this fact the laughter of his audience was explained. He really must be very funny, to see as well as to hear.

One of my main pleasures in life is in letters. Friends can't write very personal news, because they never know who will read these letters aloud to me. The reader may be a clergyman, the casual caller, or Harvey, who cleans the apartment. At any rate, letters get read, and I answer them on the typewriter.

When Dr. Bretz was living, I used to write with a pencil. He cut slots in a pasteboard that had come from the laundry in a shirt. These slots were to serve as rules to guide the lines of writing. To the pasteboard was clipped a sheet of paper, and by holding the pencil almost upright I could keep it in the slot.

After my husband's death, I was taught typing, which is much easier for my friends to read. My chief difficulty comes when I am interrupted by the telephone or the doorbell. On returning to the machine, I may not have the faintest idea of what I had been writing. Finally, I evolved the system of explaining the interruption in parentheses, and beginning a new paragraph. Receiving a letter with the word "telephone" in brackets, my son once called me up long distance, wanting to know what was the matter. He had not understood that the word in brackets meant merely an interruption in my letter writing and it took a few minutes to straighten out the difficulty. I don't make many mistakes in correspondence now, and the few that occur are easily deciphered.

Another major interest and minor activity is politics. I vote in a schoolhouse to which a friend takes me, and while she waits, three men escort me to the machine. Two of them, a Republican and a Democrat, go into the booth with me, and a Socialist stands at the open door. I tell one of the men what levers to pull down, and it is all over in the shake of a lamb's tail. No one has ever hinted that an elephant or a donkey can shake a tail so quickly. Yes, my vote is free, but not secret.

I should not, during my free years, have conceived as amusement my enjoyment of a description of a play or moving picture. But my young friend Bill vividly reproduces shows for me, while I sit comfortably at home in my wing chair. It is actually more pleasant and infinitely more convenient to see them thus. Bill possesses the art of painting pictures in words to an unusual degree. He will describe the effect of clouds on buildings, the spash of color caused by a woman's dress in the gathering dusk, a character study of a person he has watched on a Fifth Avenue bus. When Bill has finished talking, I am almost surprised to find myself still in my chair.

I wish I could tell my friends of all the entertainment they bring me, how greatly they enrich my life.

It is pleasant to think that other blind men and women who have been unable to master

Braille, and who may not have the host of friends ready to read to them that I have, do not now have to do without the joys of reading. Science and the American Foundation for the Blind have brought to them the Talking Book. To call it merely a talking book is understatement; the book not only talks but sings, and acts. It consists of a portable reading machine, similar to the phonograph in principle. The "Books" consist of a number of long-playing durable disks, which are numbered and resemble phonograph records. On these disks, trained readers from stage and radio have recorded much that is valuable and stimulating in world literature from the Book of Psalms to Alexander Woollcott. Each double-sided disk reads aloud for half an hour, and as the average novel runs to fifteen of these double-sided disks, it reads itself aloud in seven and a half hours.

As I prefer Braille, I do not use the Talking Book, but blind friends tell me that the records are now so perfect that while hearing them the medium is actually forgotten. They think of them merely as real books and forget that they are written in sound tracks and not in printed lines.

These books are recorded exclusively for the use of the blind in the sound studios of the

American Foundation for the Blind. The records are carried by the public library and are supplied free of cost.

Although the Talking Book is the most modern form in which literature reaches the reader, it harks back in spirit to medieval days. For just as the monks in the Middle Ages labored with their inks and their colors to make each volume they inscribed an individual work of art, the Foundation studies each book to be read on the disks in the effort to make it a fresh and individual adventure for the blind reader.

When I say that the Talking Books can sing, I'm thinking of the volumes of the songs of the wild birds. In them, the birds themselves have collaborated with Dr. Albert Brand of Cornell University, and their contributions range all the way from the amateur hour warblings of an immature goldfinch, to the operatic arias of the cardinal bird.

When I say the Talking Books can act, I'm thinking of one of the Foundation's more recent departures, that of bringing drama to the blind. Full casts of Broadway players now act many contemporary and classic plays for the Talking-Book disks. These disks record them as full productions, with incidental music and sound effects, with everything in fact except costumes and scenery. Even these are supplied in a way, for narrative interludes between scenes conjure up the setting, describe the costume, and make all thoroughly understandable to the blind listener.

At the time Thomas A. Edison invented the initial phonograph, using cylinder and horn with its primal squawks and squeaks, he is said to have remarked, "Here I have something which will mean a great deal to the blind." Unfortunately, Edison didn't live to see the Talking Book. But it was his invention which the American Foundation for the Blind used as the basis of its researches and experiments in developing what is claimed to be the greatest boon that science has brought to the blind in this century.

Chapter 10

It has always been my contention that everyone, man or woman, housewife or career woman, should have some particular interest unconnected with those things which go to make up the daily routine. Before I lost my sight, one of my chief interests was literature. It is still one of my great interests, but the slackening of pace necessitated by the use of Braille, the inability always to obtain the outstanding contemporary books in Braille, and the consequent dependence upon friends to read such works to me, have unavoidably curtailed my activity in that direction. Under the circumstances, it has been necessary for me to substitute other interests for those which at one time filled completely my idle hours.

Because of my own experience, my chief interest and consideration today is with the newly blinded adult. I know the life that he has lost, and I now know what his life can become. The newly blinded need a great deal of help, particularly those who have led an ordinary social life. They need not struggle through all the experiments that fell to my lot. The change we have to make is like learning to drive a car up a long hill. If there is someone with us who can show how to shift gears, taking the hill is easy. I confess that, traveling alone, I stalled the engine a number of times, but the car never turned over, nor did it slide downhill.

There really is a system about shifting gears. I talked to ophthalmologists and found them enthusiastic over my idea that a new set of mechanics in social contact can be learned. I explained to the doctors the benefits a blind person derives from society, that the new methods of walking through each day which must be employed can easily be acquired, that it was unnecessary for the blind to sit forlornly at home, and that luncheons, dinners, and teas are all possible and make life much happier. I moved my hands to illustrate for one doctor what I do with a stemmed glass, and he asked me if I could do it after a third cocktail. I had to confess that I have never tried, as one is my limit.

But to get back to my interest in the newly blinded adult. Through the late Dr. John Wheeler, I received one day an invitation to talk to the nurses at the Ophthalmological Institute.

No one had been able to induce me to talk in public during the years when I could see, and nothing short of a derrick could have put me on a platform. Yet, here, being blind, I had gladly consented, and I wondered why. The reason wasn't difficult to find. I couldn't see the audience, therefore (apparently I reasoned) the audience couldn't see me. It sounds as though one of my ancestors had been an ostrich! Then, too, I felt that I had something to say to those nurses which would be of real value. When a nurse is with a patient who is told of present blindness, or of its imminence, she is helpless to alleviate the immediate mental agony, but she may be able to shorten its duration.

Many blinded adults suffer acutely for months or years, and a dull apathy may last even longer. This later suffering is so unnecessary and so cruel that if a nurse can inject a thought of hope, plant a seed which may eventually flower, I wanted to show her how it could be done. A patient in this aloneness turns to the nearest person—the nurse.

I explained to the nurses what they might expect with some of their patients. There are those who have gone to church more or less, and consider that they know God, and who now cry out, "Why has God visited me with this affliction?" There are those who have denied God and now curse him, those who say they will commit suicide. This suicidal attitude is not confined to the blind. There are other weaklings who haven't courage to face what seems to them disaster. But people at large despise cowardice because it betrays the standards of the group, and applaud courage, which strengthens them.

There is another class of newly blind, a class of persons who may be called sit-down strikers. They give no thought to their families, and no consideration to the extra care and work they cause. They are so absorbed with themselves that they wallow in self-pity.

After mentioning these types, I gave a few practical suggestions as to the handling of a patient. Only a blind person can know of the seemingly unimportant actions that bring great comfort or discomfort.

One hint brought an immediate and delightful result, unique in my experience. I had explained that a blind person should always be spoken to before being touched, and that the nurse should say, "Here is a clean handkerchief. I'll put it in your right hand," whereas if she touches the hand without speaking it results in a nerve shock. It is easy for the normal person to imagine being touched in the dark by something unexpected. This little warning instantly bore fruit. When I was ready to leave the Institute, a soft voice said, "Here is your coat, and this is the right sleeve." I was charmed. It was my first experience of what being helped on with a coat efficiently and graciously could be. Before that, being helped on with a coat had been a muddle.

During the lecture, I stressed the importance of encouraging a blind person to use the word "blind," if only for the comfort of other people.

In my own experience in meeting new people, the word on the tip of their tongue, the one word they are afraid will slip out, is the word "blind." An innocuous expression like "blind alley" will get by the guard and there is a shocked silence. One woman said at a dinner table in response to a question by the host, "No, I couldn't do that—it would be like the blind leading the blind." The silence around that dinner table was like a feather bed dropped on the heads of the other guests. There was a little coughing and spluttering and a fresh subject was started.

I felt extremely sorry for the woman who had made the remark. She had never met me before and didn't understand the ease and frequency with which I used the word "blind." My host and hostess appreciated the situation and assured the woman that I had no sensitiveness on the subject, and later I had an opportunity when the woman came to me with an apology to explain quite fully my point of view.

I endeavor to use the word "blind" as early as possible in talking with new acquaintances. It sets them at their ease at once. It is almost possible to hear their sigh of relief, and the talk is apt to become a questionnaire, with me filling in the blanks. My circle of friends and their friends have no personal knowledge of the blind and they are eager for information.

With a new hostess I have the opportunity of setting the pace by asking for a tray or coffee table to support a cup safely, explaining in my pleasantest manner that I am not sure of holding a saucer straight. This little ceremony relieves us both; the hostess is not worried about the safety of her pretty china, and I am not thinking about my gown and can devote my attention to being as entertaining as possible.

I told this story of the coffee table to the nurses at the Ophthalmological Institute with the result that, when I was led into another room for refreshment, there was a table beside my chair.

Those nurses in the Ophthalmological Institute were delightfully responsive, and the lectures went smoothly, as did others given at New York University.

This new activity came in a rather roundabout way. The introduction to it came while I was reading Carl Carmer's "Listen to a Lonesome Drum," and fingered the word "perpendicular" several times. The use of the word in describing the position of tables struck me as odd and my curiosity was aroused. Later in the day when a visitor, who was an instructor in New York University arrived, I asked for the definition of the word, other than "vertical." This led to a discussion of what Braille did to writing and I spoke of what I call the Braille test of literature, and cited a number of examples.

The instructor, Miss Reighard, was not only interested but said that my point of view would be of value to certain classes at the university. A time was arranged for my first talk. Miss Reighard called for me and took me to Washington Square in a taxi.

Judged by the questions the students asked, Miss Reighard's idea of their interest was correct. I stressed the ease of reading words whose definition did not have to be looked up in a dictionary. I illustrated a point with the word "perpendicular," which while mathematically correct, was not so used in ordinary speech. Mr. Carmer had not been writing about mathematics but giving a description, and the youngsters caught my vision of dining tables standing on their hind legs.

The success of the first lecture led to others. I did not discuss the literary merit of a book, but stressed the fact that the test of Braille allowed no word to escape attention.

I spoke without notes, but this plan was not feasible when the University asked me to talk over the radio. There had to be a script following a general theme so that I could answer questions. I didn't try to memorize the answers. I knew the subject and talked as though I were in a living room. It may have been this feeling that made talking over the air so easy. I couldn't see the microphone and only had to remember to keep my face turned toward my right hand which lay on the table.

Now I really quite enjoy lecturing. I always feel as though I were talking to a few people, and am surprised later to learn the size of my audience. Of course, I hear the laughs scattered through the hall, and people ask questions, but these give no clue to the approximate number present. My hearers are apt to forget that I am blind, and they smile and nod and gesticulate. I am told later of these reactions, but at the time they convey nothing to me.

These little adventures into an entirely new field contributed in a valuable way to the building up of my self-confidence, and presently I found myself toying with the idea of still another adventure—the daring one of trying a vacation on my own! It was the mention by a friend of a summer vacation in the country, and the memory of long summers spent with my family away from the city in those former years when I could see, that set my mind working on the project. There were several cogent arguments against it. In the first place, not being able to see, a change of scene would have no value for me. In the second place, it was more comfortable for me to stay at home in familiar surroundings. A shift in environment meant nerve tension instead of relaxation.

Friends were always regretting my inability to leave the city during the hot weather. When leaving on their own vacations, they advised me to keep as cool as possible, to use my electric fan, to take frequent cold baths, to eat plenty of salads and ice cream. I followed their advice and passed a number of summers in my apartment with occasional breaks of short visits to the suburbs, until the enforced dullness of the season and my growing sense of self-confidence and adventure finally brought about a revolt.

I Begin Again

A sticky July day gave the final impetus to my half-formed decision concerning a vacation away from town. Even if there were no change of scene, there would be a change in my auditive horizon, and to make the change complete, I decided to choose an unknown place where there would be unknown people. The first difficulty to be overcome was how to find the place that would suit my requirements. This was settled by my friend Bill.

"I know the very spot," he said. "Beautiful country and near enough for your son to take you there in his car."

"Never mind the beauty. What about the house, can I get around in it easily?" The practical side was uppermost in my thoughts.

Bill knows my limitation both at home and in strange places. He is an excellent guide, never forgets my needs, and even while carrying on a pleasant conversation remembers to warn of steps or obstacles. Then, too, he is tall and easy to walk with. I knew that his judgment and description could be depended upon, and listened intently to his talk.

He described the old house set among trees. There were porches across the front and down both sides, the rooms were large; the stairway, easy. A bedroom near the top of the stairs and

· 151 ·

next to the bath he thought would be convenient. It sounded promising, but there were a few more questions to be asked.

"What about the people?"

"Charming. A husband and wife. You'll find them most congenial and they possess the happy faculty of letting people alone."

"Have they had any experience with a blind person?"

"No, but they are tremendously interested in what I've told them about you. They inquire after you every time I go to their house."

"The next time you go, will you ask them if they will let me come? If they think that it would be too much of a responsibility, I'll understand, nor must you feel hurt if they say 'No.' "

Bill brought back a "Yes," which gave me some insight into the character of my hostess-to-be, a bond of taking a chance on the unknown.

As Bill had foretold, the project worked smoothly. Its success was due chiefly to my host and hostess. They possessed the kindness and imagination to plan those things which are of practical assistance to a blind person. A steamer chair was placed on the porch about a foot from a screen door. Everything had been arranged so that I could reach this spot easily. A table had been taken away from a wall at the left of the stairs so that I could follow the wall with my hand. It brought me to an archway, and just inside the room a chair was placed as a guide to lead me to the fender around the hearth. From the other end of the fender there were only a few steps to the porch door. This ability on the part of persons who could see to imagine what to be blind meant was unprecedented in my experience.

Also, before I could ask for help, an outstretched hand was ready. Thanks to these people I had a sense of security, but the real magic of that sojourn was the changed auditive horizon.

A brook snored beneath my bedroom windows, a sardonic, rattling, ceaseless rhythm, irritably persistent. Never once did that brook half wake and say, "Ong! Was I snoring?" Its life was one unbroken snore. For a serenader under a window, I prefer a subway or an "el." They at least stop between trains, but a brook has no between. Fortunately I heard it only while dressing or undressing. At night I slept and my days were spent on the other side of the house. There the wind whispered, sang, and whistled through the leaves of the trees; the conferences of crickets and locusts were broken only by the shrieking protest of the blue jay.

I Begin Again

I couldn't see the doe and fawn that came one evening and stood under a tree, but was told of them. I could hear katydids gossiping over an imaginary back fence, and the hoot of an owl was a more musical warning than the siren of a police car. There was space in that auditive horizon, space for the humming bees, for the distant call of a crow, for the throaty twitter of birds at dusk, and through it throbbed the life of trees and plants.

Country sounds were so different from those in New York. Voices came clear through the air without echo; the clatter of a mowing machine compared favorably with a garbage truck. In the country, sound is seldom directly connected with people as it is in the city. Noise made by a machine indicates a human operator; cars, trucks, buses mingle their individual sounds. Subway and "el" trains throw in their separate tones. The roar rises and falls with the passing hours. I live in the midst of clamor, but the lesson learned of the benefits to be obtained from a change in my auditive horizon have never been forgotten, and now I, too, join in the talk of summer vacations.

My biggest undertaking thus far, since the loss of my sight, has been the writing of this book, and my stock of perseverance and patience has been greatly enlarged by the effort. Whatever comes next may prove easier. Many difficulties arose in the making of the book which were peculiar to my situation. There was no secretary or companion on hand to take down my ideas. It was useless for me to make notes on the typewriter, because I couldn't read them, useless to outline a chapter, because I couldn't fill it in later.

What I did do was to keep a general idea of the subject matter of a chapter in mind and write on it as fully as possible. If on completing a sentence I thought of a better construction, I wrote *xx* and followed it by the new phrase. When a single word failed to please me, one *x* was put down. To turn over a typescript written in this funny system to a copyist would have been impossible. It was evident from the beginning that I had to find someone with patience as well as intelligence to read aloud what I had written. Such a person is my friend Carol. She would read a chapter through, and as I listened I would interrupt with "not clear," "insert," at points where an idea was muddled, or where I had forgotten something. Carol would write the words in the margin and then I would have to keep the ideas in my mind and write them during the following days. Carol would then go over the chapter again and we would fit in the explanatory notes. After that she would read the chapter to me and it was ready for the first copying.

When the book was complete in this more or less sketchy but readable condition, we began the slow process of going over it sentence by sentence. This took a tremendous amount of time and I couldn't do any of it alone.

To have written in Braille would have been a still slower process for me, for while I am acquainted with the system, there has never been any occasion for me to use it. My ideas would have been lost while concentrating on the formation of individual letters. As it was, my thoughts ran faster than my fingers stuttered on an ordinary typewriter; typing not only saved my time while actually writing, but Carol could read the script.

If the writing had been in Braille, she would have had to type while I read aloud. This would have increased her work as well as mine, for her copy would have been at the point of my original typed copy, and the remainder of the work would have been the same.

Yet the time spent on the book was pleasant. It has been a diversion along my rough road.

I Begin Again

The stony path is narrow but that brings the wayside flowers closer and their fragrance helps me on my way. Sometimes it rains and the flowers are bruised and beaten to the ground, but then there is the good smell of the wet earth. The rain may sting my face but it doesn't scald like tears of self-pity.

Chapter 11

We blind can't be grouped as a class, although there may be a few fundamental generalities that apply to all. There is no typical blind person. What do we mean by "typical"? What do we mean by a typical American? We certainly don't refer to a Southern mountaineer or a slum dweller. Do we mean the American who owns his own house, has a car, and is financially secure? The differences among blind individuals are just as great, if not greater, than those among other people. We must take into consideration the age when we become blind, the cause of the blindness, and the degree of blindness, for though a person is considered industrially blind, he may possess a small degree of sight. There is a vast difference in freedom if a person can distinguish objects four or five feet in front of him or nothing at all. The person with some vision avoids objects in his path. True, he doesn't move as freely as a man with sight but he moves more comfortably than one totally blind.

The person early blinded differs radically in his mental concept of the world from an adult who becomes blind. This is true in considering even commonplace things, a room, for example. When I could see, my first sight of a room would show me its proportions, the ceiling, walls, the spacing of windows, and the waxed floor. That same glance included color, the pictures on the walls, the type of furniture, rugs, and curtains. Now that I am blind, a room means an unbounded space. There is no definite size; to put my hand on a wall will not tell me its color, its height, its length, or its decoration.

I also remember movement, which can be known only through sight, such as people walking, automobiles moving swiftly, railroad trains, even a cat or dog running. A cat is not just a warm furry bundle on my lap, nor a dog a larger animal with harsher fur.

This idea was brought to my attention by a story about a blind man whose eyes had been successfully operated on. The incident was told to me by W. G. Holmes, whose life's devotion to the blind has won our love and respect. After the operation the man went to the doctor's office for further treatment, and on his way walked through the park. One day he was laughing as he entered the office.

"What's the joke?" the doctor asked.

"I saw a dog."

"Didn't you ever see a dog before?"

"Yes, of course, but it always stood still with its head and tail down while I was feeling it. This animal was running with its head and tail up, and looked so queer that I asked a man what it was. He said it was a dog, and that made me laugh."

This blind man told the truth because he could compare the world of sight with his former blindness.

So, also, did a woman, blind from birth, who heard me speaking of the theater, and later told me that she had been very interested and could readily understand my knowing a scene through description. "I can't see it," she said, "because I've never seen anything, no gardens, no trees, no houses, or lakes." This woman is highly educated through travel and books. She may not have seen views, but she sees something infinitely better, the truth, and isn't afraid to face it. This woman, so far as I know, is unique. For, while my acquaintance with blind people is limited, the few I know, with one or two exceptions, make odd statements, and it seems incredible that they should actually believe some of the things they say.

Blind people may not want to be untruthful but some of the wild statements they make have an odd effect on their hearers. I am aware of this effect because people talk frankly to me, knowing that I am not sensitive on the subject of blindness. They repeat statements made by the blind and question their veracity. To give a satisfactory explanaion often puts me in a quandary. If blind people only realized that they can't get away with "blindman's bluff," it would make their social relations so much easier.

Their only knowledge of the real world must be gained through faulty descriptions by people who can see, or from books and the small objects that they can touch.

How can a person who has never seen even a pond, talk of a lake or conceive of an ocean? Yet a person who has seen a small body of water can mentally picture one of any size.

The inadequate information of the blind frequently produces unhappy predicaments for them. They are taught that they can do anything anyone else can do, and that there is no limitation. They also avoid the use of the word "blind," as though it were something disgraceful. I acknowledge that being blind makes life a bit awkward at times, but I use the word freely and easily.

I Begin Again

I was once asked by a blind woman if I didn't
find life more difficult as the years passed, if I
weren't often mortified and embarrassed. (Right
here, let me confess that I am often annoyed by
being addressed by a hostess through a third
person, as though my blindness carried with it
the connotation of deafness and dumbness also.
The line of reasoning and consequent deduction
are incomprehensible to me. She will invariably
ask my companion: "Does Mrs. Bretz like lemon
in tea?" Does she ever ask *me?* No! This ignoring
of a blind person's capability for hearing a question and giving an intelligent answer is a well-
nigh universal experience among blind people.)
To get back to my friend's question. I assured
her that I was never mortified, and asked her to
be more specific.

"When I stretch out my hand in the wrong
direction for a cup of tea, I feel hot all over,"
she said.

I gently explained my manner in regard to tea,
which was impossible for her to understand
because our starting points were so different. I
say that I am blind and she doesn't.

Of course the refusal to face facts is not confined
to the blind. All facts are obvious to the on-
looker sooner or later, but blindness is so easily
recognizable that it is absurd to try to conceal it.

Yet a blind woman came to call on me and in the course of our conversation objected to my use of the word "blind." She said, "If anyone referred to me as a blind girl, it would make me sick."

In refusing to acknowledge blindness, she refused to recognize the *raison d'être* of her visit, our mutual blindness, refused to recognize that the people who had sent her to me had told me that she was blind, and that I had told someone of an engagement with a blind woman. How she reconciled this attitude with the fact that she was being paid as a blind worker, and had a guide, and that she would not have had the job unless she were blind, was beyond my comprehension. I have no point of contact with such people and let them slip through my life and out.

In my observation of my fellow countrymen in the world of the blind, I find a trend that intrigues me. They make a fetish of color, and like to drag it into their conversation on every possible occasion. If the loss of eyesight is recent, and therefore the memory of color accurate, this is justified, but even then, it seems to me wise to mention this fact when talking on the subject. Otherwise those listening may acquire the entirely erroneous idea that blind people have some means of identifying color.

What they do have is a very definite associa-
tion of ideas where color is concerned, and it is
the conception of color thus acquired that is of
real interest to the seeing world.

An article in an English Braille magazine
advised blind writers to describe things as they
actually knew them; that is, the heroine's lips
as soft and warm, not scarlet; and a rose, not by
its color, pink or red, but as a blind man would
know it, a fragrant flower with thorny
stem.

One blind man said that when he heard martial
music he saw red. This seems natural, for martial
music brings the thought of marching soldiers,
war, red blood, red flags, or the hackneyed expression, "the red god of war." In the slang of today,
blue means depressed; therefore it is easy to
understand that a blind man might say that he
doesn't like blue. Of course, he doesn't know
bright blue or the blue of forget-me-nots.

A blind girl, when asked what specific colors
meant to her, said that green was naive. The idea
was probably connected with reading about
young green leaves, or an unsophisticated person
being called green.

Such items are novel to persons who can see.
What blind people think is more interesting to
me than what they do.

I Begin Again

I once heard a blind person say that the day was beautiful, and the sky bright blue. Fortunately this remark was not made in the presence of anyone with sight, because later a friend told me that the sky that day had been overcast, although the air was nice. If this friend had heard the blind man's remark and had been unaware of his lack of sight, she would have asked where he lived, as the sky here had been gray. I have been present on several such occasions and have realized the embarrassing situation, and have been told how unpleasant these scenes are for the normal person involved.

One June when I was visiting in Greenwich, my hostess took me to call on a friend of hers. The drawing room was fragrant with roses and, after we had been welcomed, I said that I smelled them and asked where they were. Our hostess led me to a bowl of roses on a near-by table. I asked about their color and if they had grown in her garden. I had had a formal rose garden some years ago and we talked of the new varieties and of the care and delight of gardens, in which all three of us were interested. The subject made a pleasant beginning of our conversation.

A butler brought in the tea and, when we were comfortably settled with cups and sandwiches, the hostess began with the familiar opening gambit, "Do you mind if I ask you a question?" Then she went on to say that a year or so before a young blind woman had been brought to her house. There had been roses in the room, as there were today, but the young woman had not behaved as I had done. On the contrary, she had exclaimed, "What lovely roses. They're pink, aren't they!" The roses were red, and the hostess looked helplessly at the guide, who shook her head and touched her lips with one forefinger. The hostess then murmured something about the roses being very fresh, but the slight pause had brought a flush to the blind girl's face. The speaker said that it was a most uncomfortable call.

If this preoccupation with color on the part of the blind is a source of surprise and bewilderment to the seeing person, the average seeing person's lack of ability to describe any given object or article is a source of equal amazement to the blind. I am impressed with this lack at almost every turn. Because I have not always been blind, a good description of something conveys a more accurate idea to me than touching it. But can I get one from my friends? No. They can describe a picture, or tell me about a magazine illustration or a moving picture because they know I can't feel such things. But if an object can be felt, descriptive power seems to lag, and after a few stumbling phrases come the familiar words: "I'll let you feel it."

The most amusing of these experiences is a description of a dress. I'm keen about styles and want to hear about fashion. There is no use in my being dubby through ignorance, at least not while I can ask questions. Therefore I will say to a friend, "Please tell me what you are wearing." Then the fun begins. The woman will bend her head to study the dress. I know this movement of the head by the change in the timbre of her voice. The dress may not be new, and even if it is, the woman certainly ought to know what it looks like. She put it on that afternoon, but she must now examine it afresh, and the following conversation takes place, the questions being mine.

"It's printed crepe." The words come slowly, hesitatingly.

"What color?"

"Oh, blue." Then with a rush, "With white and blue flowers."

"Is the background dark or light?"

"Er-kind of betwixt and between. It's sort of bright, but not really bright. I think it is serviceable."

"How is it made?"

"Two-piece skirt."

"How long is the top piece?"

"There isn't any top piece, the skirt has a seam on either side."

"What about the blouse, does it come over the skirt?"

"No, it is sewed onto the skirt. It's a pretty blouse."

"Is there a collar, and how long are the sleeves?"

My friend pauses to turn her head (again a change in voice), and apparently looks at a sleeve as though she were seeing it for the first time, and says, emphatically, "They are short."

Now short may mean a few inches below the shoulder, halfway to the elbow, or below it. I drop the subject of sleeves and ask if she wears a belt.

"Oh, yes, a scarlet one an inch wide. It's very smart."

This friend, like all the others, is unable to put herself in my place and to show me the picture I would see if I had eyesight. If I could see, my impressions would come in the following order: a bright blue dress with a scarlet belt, the approximate length of skirt and sleeves, then other details of style. Although collars are important items, I have learned not to mention them because, as the wearer can't look at them, she comes to me saying, "Feel it." To save my friends such struggles I am trying to acquire the habit of asking what other women wear. This makes it easier all around.

In my varied reading on the subject of blindness I have encountered the statement that a blind person could have no accurate conception of an object that he could not hold in his two hands. I think it was Dr. Cutsforth who wrote of a blind man feeling a replica of the statue, "Appeal to The Great Spirit," and asking if the Indian were drunk. The expression of adoration on the Indian's face was not revealed to the finger tips. This example does not mean that the sense of touch is of little value to us. Quite to the contrary, we depend on touch and hearing constantly. In my case, and in the case of all blinded adults, the sense of touch guides us around a room. We feel tables, chairs, doors, and so forth, and the thickness of rugs under our feet, but we visualize these things through memory. We cannot touch light or darkness or color. These again are memories and from knowledge we know what the words mean.

I am meticulous in referring to color before strangers, otherwise I know they will think I can observe color through touch, and apply the undeserved word "wonderful" to me. I know on what a slender foundation such a reputation is based.

A little incident took place in my home not long ago. A group of friends had already gathered before another young couple came in. At their entrance, a girl exclaimed, "That's a swell outfit you're wearing, Charlotte."

"Glad you like it. It's the first time I've worn it."

"Jade green and gold make a charming combination," I commented.

A woman gasped, "How wonderful of you to feel color vibration so quickly."

"That's a lot of hocum, Elinor. You ought to know me better by this time. The simple truth is that Charlotte described the dress to me last week, and telephoned that she was wearing it tonight."

People don't like to be debunked, but I refuse to bluff.

The careful choosing of colors for my home furnishings I take as a joke on myself, fully recognizing the absurdity. For example, when it came to having my kitchen done over, I went completely haywire and insisted on having the walls a bright yellow, sunshine or buttercup yellow, no suggestion of miserable cream. And as though that weren't enough, I had the edges of the shelves finished in black enamel, and the tops covered with scarlet oilcloth! I enjoy laughing to myself over these things. It makes life funny.

One of the best chuckles I've enjoyed had to do with the choosing of just the right shade of green for the walls of my living room. The painter had suggested apple or pea green, which I assured him were too gay for my gray hair. I'm supposed to be dignified, and there's no use advertising that I'm not always so. A more sober green would give a better impression. The difficulty lay in how to put a particular shade of color into words that a friend could understand sufficiently to get a sample of ribbon for the painter's use. I racked my memory for some object that would illustrate the color. I thought of the dark green of pine trees, the bright green of grass, the bluish green of a rye field, the yellowish green of wheat. Picturing fields, I remembered mullen. It's a lonely, aloof plant, growing singly in a pasture or abandoned field. Its tall, straight spike, topped by a scattering of miserable, puny flowers of a disreputable yellow, is decorative, though not pretty. At the base of the plant, lying close to the ground, is a whorl of fuzzy green leaves. That green was the

exact color. If mullen grows in New York, I
don't know where to telephone for it. I refused
to be daunted by this new obstacle, and began
an inquiry among my friends to find one who
might be spending a week end in the country.
The hunt was successful; the painter pinned the
leaves on the wall and matched the color.
Achievement was mine, not to mention a vast
amount of quiet amusement and entertainment!

Blindness is a very real fact, and if accepted
will not grow larger. It is never nonexistent; it
is always present. I cannot forget that I am
blind, although I don't always remember it. I
frankly accept the fact that I am not a normal
person. Although my mind and body are healthy
and four senses are active, the fifth is lacking.
Why pretend that I'm just as good as anyone
else? I certainly don't consider myself as efficient with only four senses as when I possessed
five.

Pretense is a stumbling block in the free inter-
course between the blind and people with all
five senses, and the blind are to blame. They try
to insist on being treated like other people. They
refuse to acknowledge the necessity of guides,
of the helping hands all along their journeys,
although they use them all. It isn't needful to
whine over our condition, but why be com-

bative? It is easier for everyone if we behave naturally, doing as much as we can, as quickly as we can with safety, and being grateful for the help given us so freely.

Gratitude is a virtue; Disraeli said it is the rarest. It is something we can possess if we want to. My appreciation of others fills life with joy. I've known people since childhood, but never until I became blind did I know such universal kindness.

In talking with one of my friends about appreciation, I mentioned how much trouble we blind caused other people. Margaret strongly objected to this statement, and declared that I was never any trouble.

"Stop and think a minute," I said. "When you invite me to dinner, which you are going to cook, you must prepare the food, probably leaving something on the stove that won't burn while you are collecting me. You change from house to street clothes, and allow three-quarters of an hour for the round trip. When we reach your apartment you change back to house clothes and serve dinner. The process of dressing is repeated when I am ready to go home."

"That isn't any more trouble than remembering to have fish for my Catholic friends on Friday."

"Nonsense," I laughed. "You are such a good hostess that you always remember a guest's taste and never once served tomatoes to me."

She ignored my protest. "I like to cook and frequently have friends to dinner."

"Quite true, but you don't expend energy and three quarters of an hour at the beginning and end of each evening on other people, only on me. You don't have to collect your other guests, and you must not deprive me of appreciating such courtesy. You're a sweet girl." One thing about being blind, I can't see a person blush.

She said that it was no trouble to walk a few blocks, that in the city it was the only thing to do. She went on to say that in her home town everyone had a car and collecting friends was the custom.

"It's no use, Margaret, if everyone had a car your guests would come in their own. But what use would a car be to me? I would always have to be sent for. Suppose your husband had come home from the office, planning to water the garden, and changed into old clothes before you could tell him that he had to go for me. Imagine his state of mind. He would probably growl because you didn't tell him sooner. And if you had told him the minute he got home, he would look at the garden, loaf around for fifteen or twenty minutes, and way down inside he would have said, 'Oh, hell,' because you would have pretended to be horrified if he had let it slip out. My vanity doesn't want anyone to say, 'Oh, hell,' in regard to me—even way down inside.''

Margaret giggled, ''All the same you shouldn't feel badly about it.''

The truth is that I don't feel badly in the least, but I do appreciate people's kindness, because they have made an effort and devoted time and thought to giving me pleasure.

The essential ''me'' is not changed since blindness. It is the outside world that has wrought the miracle, or my new experience with and relationship to the outside world.

I have experienced kindness and had dear friends through the years. But now everyone I meet adds to my thanksgiving. No one is too poor, none too humble, to give me kindly words or acts. It's a nice old world, if you see it with blind eyes. There is nothing crooked, nothing mean, nothing selfish.

Each blind individual can have this experience if he wants to, and there are those who do have it, thank God.

Sometimes blind people say to me that I am lucky.

I am not.

My philosophy works, that's all. And it is practical enough to help others.

Among the earliest tasks for a blind person, particularly a woman, is the conquering of the fear of being left alone. This fear is not necessarily a concomitant of blindness. Many women have it, and actually pride themselves on its cultivation.

My mother had this quality, and I was cognizant of it as a child. Mother would never enter a dark room. Someone would be sent in to light the gas. Father may have thought her timidity a charming and womanly trait, but we children didn't. Every night in the eighty-two years of Mother's life, she spent several hours in trembling fear of burglars—thousands of hours of terror, over something that never happened. Nor have I ever encountered a marauder, although once in my life since I became blind I suspected nefarious designs. This was only two or three years ago. I was awakened by the sound of two men talking in low tones in front of my bedroom window. They apparently were standing on the fire escape. Burglars? I slipped quickly out of bed and hurried to the living room, where I felt the hands of the clock. Quarter after nine. It was morning, I knew, because I had gone to bed at midnight. The month was May. It must be broad daylight.

Later the superintendent told me that the men were house painters, examining the window casings! I was glad I hadn't screamed.

There are awkward moments for a blind person living alone, but we can't afford fear. Fear is an emotion that must be combated.

Life is full of fighting. One of my struggles was to face the fact of blindness and the knowledge that life had to begin again. Blindness isn't the only trouble in the world, nor has it been my only trial. And to begin again is always possible. In a way, each day offers an opportunity to begin again. And there is a way to begin.

Whatever your trouble, whatever your tragedy, face it squarely. You may not be able to conquer it, but don't let it conquer you. Physical life, for the individual, begins at birth, but "living" begins at any time, with no age limit. The time to begin it is today.

Instead of wringing our hands and bemoaning what we cannot help, let each person do his bit to make other people happy by putting himself in order, and then his house. It is about all we commonplace folk are capable of.

The way to put yourself in order is to take stock of your assets and liabilities.

Be as honest about your liabilities as your assets; in other words, don't excuse your mistakes and praise your virtues.

It isn't necessary to tell other people what you have discovered about yourself. Above all, keep that knowledge as a private possession. It then becomes an asset. If you tell others, it becomes a liability.

No outsider is really interested in your private struggles or your inner personal affairs. They may appear to listen, but unfortunately the basis of their sympathy is usually curiosity.

It is also unwise to form the habit of believing that everything, including yourself, is perfect because you desire it to be. If you practice this method of thinking, some day a little common sense will make you realize what a fool you have been making of yourself.

Common sense will point out that there are evils and ills in the world, and that your business is to conquer them, first in yourself, and then, when you are strong, you may be able to help others. Your strength is nurtured by noble ideas, garnered from good books and from good people. Faith is of invaluable assistance.

My faith in God is a help and comfort; it has become an integral part of me. It encourages and sustains me. We all need a strengthening of the spirit.

There is no rule of thumb for right thinking, no universal panacea to give happiness.

The limitations imposed by blindness have made it necessary for me to develop a sense of pleasure. My life is a little garden with only space enough to grow a small number of flowers. How foolish it would be to refuse to grow two or three plants because I can't have an estate where a thousand flowers could bloom. It would be still more foolish to let my garden run to weeds, or to trample the earth hard and bare by pacing up and down in an agony of self-pity. To cherish and rejoice over my few flowers gives me unspeakable joy.

My joy in life is incomprehensible to new acquaintances. One woman exclaimed, "You won't acknowledge you're blind."

"On the contrary," I said, "it is because of my acknowledgement that I can find any pleasure at all."

She protested vehemently, "No, you want to go on doing the things you've always done."

"Quite true," I agreed, "but most of my desires cannot be fulfilled and many of my tastes remain unsatisfied. Therefore, those that are left have an enhanced value. When I do something successfully, a thing so commonplace to you as to be unnoticed, my pleasure is not only in the accomplishment but also in the doing."

People actually say to me, "You don't seem to have any troubles." They say this with my blind face before their eyes as well as other facts of an unpleasant nature. It seems to me that many people absolutely refuse to recognize disagreeable truths, believing that by so doing the facts shrink to nothingness. There are other people who say that thinking of me makes their own troubles shrink.

Another odd idea is that my disposition, as my nose, has developed without conscious effort on my part. I deny this. It requires persistence and determination to acquire cheerfulness. I do not mean "always looking on the bright side." I mean being able to look on the dark side and to say with a laugh, "You can't hurt me." For the dark side is the inside and that we can overcome and control.

Some persons practice the replacement of a bad thought by a good one. They quote, "Nature abhors a vacuum." When an idea comes to me, I examine it, and if I don't like its looks I wring its neck and toss it into the discard. And I leave the rest to Nature. I don't consciously try to find a better idea. *Chacun à son goût.* There is no value in spending time in useless regret. What is done is done and to keep it alive in the present does no good and makes us unhappy. Trying to relive the past, wondering if we had done differently whether results would have been different, is like playing over a bridge hand, and that often causes a row.

Live today the things of today and don't consider that we are important to anyone but ourselves. Blindness has taught me to face facts, to enjoy little things, to appreciate people, and to laugh at myself.

So I just keep on facing facts. It's surprising how many of these pesky things crop up. They occupy a great deal of time, and on occasions they afford amusement. In any case, they have to be faced.

I have given up trying to anticipate what may be in wait around the corner. There seem to be no corners in my immediate vicinity, and I trudge along, day by day, without wasting time over wondering about the length of the road. I have an inward peace that is never shaken by outward difficulties.

I have found happiness, and, what is more, I appreciate it.

Chapter 12

Sight has been called the queen of the senses and the loss of it is a living tragedy.

An adult has depended on his eyes for education, for his work and play, and as a guide in every action. We can scarcely estimate our almost complete dependence on sight until we have lost it. I know from my own experience.

The horrors of the first hours of blindness, the knowledge of its irrevocability, have never been erased. There is no escape from blindness, it confronts me at every turn, every motion. I have learned to accept its enforced limitations, to make what I can out of what is left, but never for one moment is it forgotten.

One of my early difficulties arose from believing the myths in regard to blindness. I was told of the many wonderful things blind people did, but no one even insinuated that in accomplishing these things the blind person had been aided by a devoted pair of eyes.

I Begin Again

Eagerly I had accepted all these stories, trying some of them out for myself—and fell with a dull thud. I not only could not do any of them, I couldn't even approach doing them. To acknowledge my failure and not to lose courage to go on was a severe test.

It was at this period that I began to think an action through before attempting it. It was later that I learned that most of the clever things that blind people did were not done alone. My fault was perhaps that I had tried to do them unaided. But the attempt taught me my own capabilities and my own limitations, the one as important as the other.

My days are made up of tiny happenings, and with them I have woven my life's pattern. The weaving is uneven, often cramped and pinched, but I still go on and the design grows better. I am able to laugh and play at adventure. Childish some of it, undoubtedly, because I must make my own fun, within such narrow limits.

My day is full of little things and if my mental attitude toward them is pleasant, the day is filled with enjoyment. It's nice for my left hand to feel smooth, dustless furniture, or to discover a spot that has escaped the dustcloth in my right hand. There is a satisfaction in knowing that a job, no matter how commonplace, has been done to the best of my ability. I must put up with many halfway performances, so that one really well done gives me added satisfaction.

Of course, it takes time to keep my apartment in order, but the time is pleasantly spent and complimentary remarks on my housekeeping are gratifying. I know it isn't perfect, but also know that I have done my best.

Telephone calls are pleasant, too. I like the excited ring of the bell, for even a wrong number is a voice from the outside world. When I want to make a call, I dial operator and give her my number and also the one I want. This is a service given by the telephone company to the blind. The numbers I use infrequently I have written in Braille so that it isn't necessary to wait until someone is here to look them up in the directory. The telephone is not only a help but a distinct pleasure.

Through the years of blindness and today, I have been and still am an avid collector of experiences. In the early years they came so fast they could only be laid aside for future consideration. My mind was an attic where things were left to be sorted out at a later date, and there was also the discard heap.

The discard heap is big and if a junkman carted it away a new heap would soon form. It might not grow so fast as in the early days of blindness, but part of the day's routine is to throw away, regretfully, some desire, great or small.

The discard heap is not raked over or its objects allowed to cause me heartache. The discard heap is a gone-forever-pile and life goes on.

The real opportunity for so sorting and cataloguing came when I wanted to put my experiences in words. In the attic I found things that had long been forgotten. The present has always been too full for me to mull over the past, but it has been amusing to compare my early struggles with what I do now.

The things we learned in babyhood, to walk, to stretch out our hands for desired objects, to recognize people, do not consciously remain in our memory. We have formed many habits before we begin to think and plan. A newly blinded adult must in practice go back to babyhood and learn everything afresh, with the extra difficulty of being hampered by years of habit.

My experiences are not unique. I had to learn to walk, to learn to feel for a desired object, to learn to recognize people by the sound of their voices. The casting out of former habits is perhaps more difficult than the acquiring of new ones. Thrusting aside the old way and concentrating on the new produces a mental strain that tires me physically.

The necessity for undivided attention probably belongs to the babyhood era. I can't walk across a room safely and talk to a visitor at the same time. When a sprained ankle put me on crutches, I couldn't concentrate on the secure placing of their tips and remember my balance. I had to engage a companion, support myself by one arm over her shoulders and a crutch under the other arm. It was pretty awkward and, as soon as possible, I shifted to a stout Malacca stick which belonged to my son.

I think that it is safe to say that no action has become automatic; no matter how inconsequential it may seem, it requires concentrated thought. I can't do one thing and think about something else while doing it. I can't even walk safely to the telephone and think about the number to be called. I have learned through bumps to think only of what I am doing, and to wait until seated in the chair by the telephone before putting my mind on the desired number.

I can't remember to keep my nose out of a book and friends who have watched me read, say that my head moves from side to side as though my eyes were following my reading finger. It's a silly useless habit, which still persists, because I am intent on what I am reading and don't think about my head. I've tried to hold my head high and, figuratively speaking, "Look at the ceiling," only to find that my reading finger stops moving. Even in so small an action my thoughts can't be divided. If I had never read by eyesight, it would be easy to sit comfortably with my head resting on the back of a chair and let my finger travel across the open book in my lap. The old habit of looking at a page persists, however, with a resultant crick in the back of my neck. I always look with blind eyes at what my hands are doing and to call myself a dumb egg doesn't alter the habit.

There is nothing to help my hands while I am smoking. My blind eyes try to watch the end of a cigarette when I am lighting it, although the middle finger of my left hand is there to feel the heat of the match or electric lighter, and my careful observation doesn't prevent an occasional scorch. I am intellectually aware of the folly of trying to see, but go right on doing it.

I know that I can't see and the struggle to supply a substitute from the remaining four senses for the lost one of sight puts me on my mettle.

The belief that we blind have a sixth sense or that in compensation our other senses are keener is disproved by searching scientific tests. Yet the erroneous belief continues to be widely held.

As a matter of fact, however, tests have repeatedly shown that not only are our other senses *not* keener but they are *frequently less keen* than those of people who can see.

I find a thrill in outwitting a difficulty, a smug so-there-now feeling that lightens what might otherwise be a drab existence.

When I hear of an adult who has lost his sight and who sits down to wallow in self-pity, I want to hold out my hands and say, "Come, friend, let me help you find a new life. Let me guide you in this strange world, and show you the treasures that are within yourself."

Why, oh, why will people not try another way when one has failed? It is not only true of the blind, it is also true of other people. Each day everyone has a chance to begin again. What was yesterday's mistake—a quarrel, a failure, a desire ungratified? All right, yesterday is past. Today is here to begin again; don't waste precious time in mourning. Spend it in building.

I know the heartbreaking difficulty of digging a foundation, but others have done it and so can you. The strength you have acquired, the resolution that has forced you to drill through rock, will enable you to build a house you will enjoy living in.

I dug away the sand of discouragement shovelful by shovelful. Sometimes the shovel wasn't really full, but persistent effort finally found the rock of courage. Courage has been a firm foundation stone, for when the winds of adversity have whipped up a gale, my little house has stood solid. Courage is here for everyone and all a man has to do is to wield his own shovel, while we who know the value of what he seeks are ready to lend a helping hand and cheer him on.

The labor involved develops persistence and the will to succeed, and these in time come into daily practice. They have aided me to learn new lessons, little things such as finding my way around a room, managing forks and spoons, dressing myself. In retrospect these accomplishments seem trifling, but they were the first efforts of putting into practice the will to succeed, and each tiny success brought a song to my heart. Later on I attempted bigger things, always with courage and the song that makes life gay.

The making of friends requires courage, particularly for us who are blind. We must put our pride in our pocket and the pocket must be capacious enough to contain many social amenities. We know that we appear awkward and must not appear to mind it.

Our only claim, if claim it can be called, on the tolerance of other people, is by forgetting first their pity and then by forgetting our own troubles in the understanding of theirs. Our own misfortune is so obvious that it isn't worth mentioning. Our inside song, the song that bubbles out in laughter and shows itself in the tone of our voice, is all that is demanded of us. This doesn't require conscious effort if we have courage and live with the song, particularly when alone. It is present in our manner and our words.

I have been a bit surprised at the comments I've received from blind people on my cheerfulness, and they pacify themselves by saying that life has been easy for me! It is useless to argue this point.

Friends contribute a large share of joy and entertainment to my days. They come to me more often than I go to them, and provide new ideas and fresh interests for me to mull over after their visits. When I hear of a person without friends, I know that the remedy lies within himself.

Next to friends and books, my chief amusement lies in my present condition. This is a cultivated point of view which is not artificial, for it has grown through my experiments. There is fun, after washing the coffeepot, to have my fingers hunt out a tricky ground hiding away with the expectation of joining the next making. I toss him into the sink and float him down the drain alone. His companions had been thrown into the garbage can en masse. The fate of the naughty ground being unobserved, another ground, sometimes two or three, will play the same game. They are unoriginal in their choice of a hide-out and are quickly found.

There is amusement, too, when a new acquaintance on going to the china closet exclaims that the dishes are clean. Did she fancy that I ate off dirty plates and drank out of unwashed cups? Funny idea.

Underneath, and woven through all these activities, is the conviction that I am playing a part, that at any moment my role will be changed. It is incredible that I should be blind. It is some hideous puzzle that must be solved. Despite the fact that I have accepted blindness, I am conscious of this other feeling, which never leaves me. I argue unsuccessfully that the idea comes from my years of sight and the living memory of those years, but it doesn't convince me the least bit.

Most roads are stony and beset with pitfalls. I have managed to make a game of the obstacles, the difficulties, the inconvenience and frustrations that beset my path to where I could begin again. It was not accomplished in a day. It takes constant effort, but it can be done. And if I who walked that road can help others to take it more easily and quickly, I shall feel that the writing of this message has not been in vain.

Without my faith in God, I doubt that I should have been able to travel that road myself with any degree of success. It is a faith that has been my sure guide for many years, one which I am glad to say was acquired before blindness assailed me.

Religious forms are among my earliest memories as a small child. My family took me to church because it was the proper thing to do. Everyone went to church in the eighties and nineties. There were two churches within a few blocks of our house, one a Presbyterian, the other, Episcopal. At twenty minutes after ten on Sunday morning we joined a procession of neighbors that filled the street. We attended the Episcopal church, where our family occupied a large pew. The service was mostly music, and I liked that. The boy choir sang all the responses and the clergyman did the rest. We were allowed to join softly in the hymns, but the top notes were always too high for me, so I just listened.

After the morning service we again joined the procession of neighbors, this time homeward bound, all of us eager for the large midday dinner. Vespers at four o'clock was not obligatory. Father and Mother never went and I didn't go until I was fifteen. I liked this service because so many of my young friends were there. The choir sang, the sermon was short, and we were back home in an hour.

We looked forward to Sunday-night supper, which was a pleasant meal with some of our young friends always present. We weren't allowed to play or sing secular music, and we weren't the hymn-singing variety. However, we managed to make a great deal of noise with "There is a Green Hill" and others of its kind. "The Lost Chord" was also permissible, perhaps because of the amen motif. One Sunday amusement that was not curtailed was the reading of secular books; the neighbors couldn't hear us reading.

The regular churchgoing of my girlhood stopped after I was married. Religion had never seemed necessary to me personally, although I knew that it was of interest to many people. My chief interest was in the people themselves and I read ancient religions and modern cults because of their influence on their followers. It was all pretty solemn. Nowhere did I find an explanation of my own experiences in the joy and beauty of life, of laughter and color and friendship.

I found the answer years later in the Christian faith, a living, vital faith which had nothing in common with the formal religious practice of my girlhood.

An example of this living faith which I keep as an inspiring memory was the reaction of an Irish girl whose brother had come over to New York. Their aunt gave a party for them and when the two arrived at the apartment, dancing was already going on. The girl ran to a bedroom to take off her hat and coat. Minutes passed and as she did not return her aunt went to find her. She found the girl on her knees, and asked what she was doing. She explained, "I'm thanking God, because I'm so happy. I was afraid I'd forget when I got dancing." A prayer of thanksgiving is the one most of us are apt to forget. We remember to ask God for things but seldom remember to thank Him for what He has already given us.

The thanksgiving attitude of mind was exemplified for me in a charming couple I met several years before I became blind. The wife's invitation to visit them was gladly accepted, and I found the husband and wife even more charming and gay in their own home than at our first meeting. Their two sons were jolly little fellows. The parents were Anglo-Catholics and practiced their religion in their everyday life at everyday chores, and the house was full of laughter and happiness.

It was so astonishing that my questions were numerous and probably a bit personal. Nevertheless, they understood and answered sympathetically. I have visited homes where there were many servants and beautiful gardens, and there has been no envy in my heart of my hostess' possessions and no desire to emulate their lives. But here was something different. These people showed me a new aspect of life. Their faith was not merely a cornerstone, it was the entire edifice. The vital glow of their life and their interesting conversation have made of that visit a beloved memory. I am glad to say that these people remain my very good friends, and what I learned from them was a great help when blindness fell on me.

When anyone suggests that my blindness is a Divine visitation, I am horrified at their conception of God. Such an idea is barbaric. A human father who blinded his child for any reason whatsoever would be lynched by the neighbors, and their only regret would be that they had not done it sooner. The concept of a Heavenly Father being more cruel than a human father is repugnant to me. I do not blame God for my blindness. It is the consequence of my ignorance. But God helps me, as my Father.

I am not disturbed over the way other people find God, nor am I worried about my faith being orthodox or unorthodox. My faith is simple and sure. Our Lord is our friend. And just as a dear friend here on earth adds to our pleasure, helping in the daily tasks, talking to us, or going with us to parties, so the presence of the Lord adds to our joy.

I have purposely mentioned parties, for to me an important lesson, and one to be remembered, is that the first miracle took place at a wedding feast. Our Lord was a welcome guest. He didn't look with disapproving eyes on the merriment of the other guests; indeed He contributed to the success of the party. He had the courage to mingle with different classes of people and did not confine Himself to a few chosen friends. He didn't criticize His neighbors or offer them gratuitous advice. He helped them when they asked Him. It is a great inspiration and comfort to know that He lived the ordinary everyday life of men. He experienced hunger and weariness and the inner torment, "His soul was heavy within Him." This knowledge helps through the arid spots of life.

Now I get to church only once or twice a year, but the Church never forgets me, and every week sends its representative. The clergyman combines his priestly office and friendship in an agreeable whole. After a short service he will talk or read something that he thinks will interest me. It may be a religious book, good fiction, or poetry. His choice is varied and entertaining.

It is amusing to notice the effect of the clergy on my agnostic friends. They are astounded to find a real man in a man of the cloth. One such encounter caused an agnostic to say, "He's a damn charming fellow." I have been fortunate in my contact with the clergy. Old and young, they have proved themselves wise, considerate, and understanding. They always ask me if there is anything that they can do for me. They go downstairs and bring up my mail and read the letters to me. They address the letters that I have written, and mail them. They open jars and bottles that baffle me, and do numerous other little chores. They don't think of their dignity but of Christ. They don't talk about humility; they live it.

One of the young Episcopal priests comes to my Christmas party and doesn't object in the least to being announced as "one mug." The explanation of this apparently rude appellation is that my son serves wassail in mugs, and Carol, who lets the guests in by the back door, looks down the stairs and announces how many persons are arriving by calling the number of mugs to be prepared. This little unceremonious ceremony makes the guests laugh.

Actual churchgoing is not necessary to my simple faith. Controversial issues of the churches have no place in it. Theological discussions and ecclesiastical formulas are outside its functioning. I am not a mystic, and if God talked to me in the silence, I should think that my imagination created the message. God knows this and uses people to show me His love and care. I feel these through the kindly act, an encouraging word, a gift, and accept people as God's messengers. When I thank a person I am also thanking God.

It is this attitude that makes kindness such an important factor in my life. The superintendent of the apartment house, who carefully watches the people coming to see me, plays the role of guardian angel, although he would be very much surprised to learn of it. The special care and attention shown me in restaurants and shops is not bought with money, it is God's smile.

This fact is the explanation of my happiness and gaiety despite what people call the tragedies of my life. There is no tragedy in happiness, nor sorrow in gaiety. Life for me is made up of little things that contribute to joy and comfort. I don't need to ask God to gratify some special desire. If he wants me to have it, it comes through a person.

The quiet hours of my day have a joyousness of their own. My faith in God fills the still places in my heart. To think of Him, of something He said, perhaps only a word, is a sure inspiration. The thought applies directly to some present need and gives me strength to go on. Peace fills my soul. "My peace I give unto you," and the "you" is me! Life becomes smooth; my troubled mind grows calm.

I may have been thinking over a problem, trying to work it out, and the solution isn't clear. I've gone as far as possible and put the way up to God. His help has never failed. I am so sure of it that it seems only fair for me to do as much as possible for myself, to struggle as best I can, and when confronted by a stone wall, to ask God for wisdom and understanding to show me what to do. There are not only help and comfort in God's friendship, but also a deep joy.

One of His gifts is a deepened appreciation of the kindness of the world. No one can take appreciation from us, for we blind have more opportunity to put it into practice than others. Appreciation may be the first step toward gratitude, and gratitude is in our hearts, is like a fire newly lighted in a cold hearth. It warms us through and through and makes our own living happier. We can also share this warmth with others, for we blind have a place in society which it is in our power to make an important place. People like to talk to us because we hold our heads high and are not bowed beneath our troubles.

The result of my religious reading has brought me to the conclusion that the essential necessity is friendship with God. There is a verse in the Old Testament which begins, "Acquaint now thyself with Him and be at peace." It is as simple as that. We can become acquainted with God. He is ever ready to be our friend; all we have to do is to want His friendship and try to understand.

Our desire is the chief and strongest part; understanding comes more slowly, and to each one of us it comes differently. When we consider a human friend, we know that it gives us pleasure to say and do things that will please him. We can use this same attitude toward God. We like to think about Him, to talk to Him, to feel that He is near. We know that He understands our desire, understands our mistakes and the daily occupations that distract our minds.

It is difficult to put this feeling into words. I tried to once and my listener interrupted with an exclamation, "You shock me the way you talk about God. You talk as though He were a friend."

"I hope He is," was my answer.

To this person, God was a far-off potentate whose wrath must be appeased by prayer and supplication. Of course we feel humble and small in the presence of All Wisdom, Power, and Understanding. Just as a little child feels small and powerless and *safe* in his father's arms.

Yes, there is evil and sorrow and trouble in the world, but in that trouble and sorrow there is also God's friendship. He does "lead me through the valley of the shadow." How can I be afraid?